Occupy Religion

Religion in the Modern World

Series Advisors
Kwok Pui-lan, Episcopal Divinity School
Joerg Rieger, Southern Methodist University

This series explores how various religious traditions wrestle with the dynamic and changing role of religion in the modern world and examines how past changes reflect on today's critical issues. Accessibly and engagingly written, books in this series will look at secularization, global society, gender, race, class, and sexuality and their relation to religious life and religious movements.

Titles in the Series

Not God's People: Insiders and Outsiders in the Biblical World by Lawrence M. Wills
The Food and Feasts of Jesus: Inside the World of First Century Fare, with Menus and Recipes by Douglas E. Neel and Joel A. Pugh
Occupy Religion: Theology of the Multitude by Joerg Rieger and Kwok Pui-lan

Occupy Religion

Theology of the Multitude

Joerg Rieger and Kwok Pui-lan

ROWMAN & LITTLEFIELD PUBLISHERS, INC.
Lanham • Boulder • New York • Toronto • Plymouth, UK

Published by Rowman & Littlefield Publishers, Inc.
A wholly owned subsidary of The Rowman & Littlefield Publishing Group, Inc.
4501 Forbes Boulevard, Suite 200, Lanham, Maryland 20706
www.rowman.com

10 Thornbury Road, Plymouth PL6 7PP, United Kingdom

British Library Cataloguing in Publication Information Available

Library of Congress Cataloging-in-Publication Data

Rieger, Joerg.
Occupy religion : theology of the multitude / Joerg Rieger and Kwok Pui-lan.
p. cm. — (Religion in the modern world).
Includes index.
ISBN 978-1-4422-1791-1 (cloth : alk. paper) — ISBN 978-1-4422-1793-5 (electronic)
1. Social justice—Religious aspects. 2. Occupy movement. 3. Protest movements—United States—
History—21st century. 4. Public opinion—United States. I. Kwok, Pui-lan. II. Title.
BL65.J87R54 2012
201'.7—dc23
2012023527

Printed in the United States of America

Contents

Acknowledgments

In the process of writing this book, we were grateful to many individuals and institutions for their generous help and support. We want to thank the faculty, staff, and students of the Episcopal Divinity School, Perkins School of Theology, Southern Methodist University, and a group of graduate students from Harvard University and Boston College for stimulating conversations and for pointing us to helpful books, articles, newspapers, and websites. Professor Christopher Duraisingh was an important dialogical partner, especially for the chapter on the church. We are grateful to Professors Yung Suk Kim, Benny Liew, and Zayn Kassam, as well as Rosemarie Henkel-Rieger and others who have passed along relevant information about resources and websites. We want to acknowledge those colleagues and friends who have responded and commented on Facebook and a blogpost sent out to solicit feedback.

We are much indebted to the following individuals for taking the time to be interviewed and agreeing to be in conversation with us for this book. They have participated in the Occupy movement in different cities of the United States: John Allen, Matthew Arlyck, Thomas M. Beaudoin, Rita Nakashima Brock, Brendan Curran, Getzel Davis, Edmund Harris, Hannah Hofheinz, Sarah Monroe, Erica Richmond, Cat Salonek, Stephanie Shockley, CB Stewart, Ryan Wallace, and Jennifer Wilder. We were able to share some of the ideas of the book at the American Academy of Religion and with the faculty, students, and community of the Academy of Religion of the College of Wooster in Ohio, Fordham University in New York, and Hamline University in Minnesota, and received very useful feedback. We want to thank the Rev.

Linda Morgan-Clement and the Rev. Nancy Victorin-Vangerud, as well as Professors Thomas M. Beaudoin, Charles Kammer, and Deanna Thompson, for their hospitality during our visit. We want to thank participants in the Occupy movement who keep us grounded in the kinds of things that matter and the grassroots organizations with which we work, including North Texas Jobs with Justice, the Dallas-area Workers' Rights Board, and Pacific, Asian, and North American Asian Women in Theology and Ministry.

Sarah Stanton, acquisitions editor at Rowman & Littlefield, was with us when we first discussed the book project. She has been an unfailing source of support from the beginning and helped shepherd the manuscript through the process. We offer thanks to Patricia Stevenson and the staff at Rowman & Littlefield, who have worked on this project with care and professionalism. We also want to acknowledge the tremendous help offered by Susan Spilecki in editing the manuscript. We are likewise very grateful to Spencer Bogle for preparing the index with meticulous care and efficiency, and to Catherine Owens for her assistance in proofreading. Thanks are also due to the Episcopal Divinity School and the Perkins School of Theology for providing research assistance and research funds. Last but not least, we thank our families for their warmth and steadfast support and for the joy they have brought to our lives.

Chapter One

Why Occupy Religion?

We'll occupy the streets
We'll occupy the courts
We'll occupy the offices of you
Till you do
The bidding of the many, not the few
We are the many
You are the few
—"We Are the Many," Makana

As the multitude filtered into lower Manhattan and eventually into Zuccotti Park in New York, excitement was in the air. They came from all walks of life to express their anger and disgust that American banks worked for the rich and the political system was broken. Some young protesters brought their sleeping bags, believing that they could spend the night on Wall Street. Marina Sitrin, an activist, recalled, "That was an incredible moment."[1] Sitrin and other activists in New York had worked tirelessly over the summer months to organize the protest. Just as the civil rights movement was a defining moment for the older generation, the Occupy Wall Street movement could well be a turning point for the young men and women gathered under the clear sky on this September night.

The protest was inspired by a small Canadian-based magazine, *Adbusters*, which issued a call in July for people to "flood into lower Manhattan, set up tents, kitchens, peaceful barricades and occupy Wall Street for a few months." Local organizers in New York met to plan for action and set up a website: occupywallst.org.[2] On September 17, 2011, some one thousand protesters streamed into Zuccotti Park, north of the New York Stock Exchange, to denounce big banks, big corporations, and government bailouts. Images of the red, grey, and green tents in the Occupy Wall Street encampment went viral across the globe. On October 15, 2011, protests, rallies, and demonstrations took place in more than 950 cities around the world, showing that Occupy Wall Street had touched a deep chord.

The Occupy movement was part of a much larger global protest and revolt in 2011. It began when a Tunisian fruit vendor, Mohamed Bouazizi, drenched himself in paint thinner and then lit a match to protest against police harassment and government callousness. His death ignited large-scale rallies and demonstrations for democracy and economic justice across Arab cities in Tunisia, Egypt, Libya, Syria, Bahrain, Yemen, Algeria, and other countries. Some three hundred thousand protesters occupied Tahrir Square and the adjacent streets in Cairo for eighteen days from January to February and finally brought down the Egyptian president Hosni Mubarak. Journalists and commentators used the term "Arab Spring" to describe the populist uprisings across North Africa and the Middle East, although not all the protesters were Arab. Encouraged by political populism in the Arab world, *Adbusters* issued a challenge for Americans: "Are you ready for a Tahrir moment?"

Time magazine chose "The Protester" as its 2011 Person of the Year, saying, "In 2011, protesters didn't just voice their complaints; they changed the world."[3] The year 2011 was another year of economic crises across the globe, after the financial market plummeted in 2008. In early August, Standard & Poor's downgraded the U.S. credit rating for the first time, dealing a symbolic blow to the world's economic superpower. The debt crises in Greece, Portugal, Italy, and Spain brought about the near collapse of the Euro. Many European governments had no other choice except to tighten their belts and adopt austerity measures. People responded with swift and fierce reactions. On May 15, 2011, twenty-thousand *indignados*, "the outraged," poured into Madrid's Puerta del Sol plaza, along with tens of thousands more in other Spanish cities. One of their slogans said, "We are not goods in the hands of politicians and bankers."

These mass protests sprang up without much encouragement from the established political parties. The protesters were predominantly young, educated, and middle class. They were frustrated by welfare cuts, rising student debts, unemployment, and the dysfunctional political and economic systems. Instead of resigning themselves to hopelessness, they used social networks and the Internet to find other like-minded people and took to the street to denounce capitalism and demand radical changes. Occupy Wall Street declares, "2011 will be remembered as a year of revolution, the beginning of the end for an unsustainable global system based on poverty, oppression, and violence."[4]

Global movements for economic justice began as protests during the annual meetings of the International Monetary Fund (IMF) and the World Bank in different European cities in the late 1980s. Anti-globalization efforts gathered momentum in 1999 in Seattle, when demonstrators blocked the delegates' entrance to the World Trade Organization (WTO) meetings. Protest groups joined hands to bring the plight of farmers, fishing people, small businesses, and indigenous peoples to public attention during WTO, G7, and G20 gatherings. In addition to protesting economic inequity, global efforts to denounce the Iraq War culminated in massive demonstrations in numerous cities over the weekend of February 15, 2003. The protest in Rome involved 3 million people, while the rally in Madrid attracted 1.5 million. The Occupy movement represents the latest expression of the movement of the multitude. Its slogan—"We are the 99 percent"—captures the imagination of people who believe that the status quo is unjust and unsustainable and that a new social contract is urgently necessary.

Mainstream media in the United States at first ignored the Occupy movement, paying it little attention. Some journalists dismissed the occupiers as nothing more than a bunch of homeless people and privileged students. But when politicians, including President Barack Obama, started to take notice and weighed in, the media gave greater coverage to it. The occupiers learned from other movements in Tunisia, Egypt, and Iran to use social media and live video streaming to broadcast their message. The movement created its websites, anthems, songs, symbols, slogans, videos, and livestream broadcasts via the Internet. With 2012 being an election year in the United States and the unemployment rate hovering around 8 percent, the question of how to fix the economy has become a focal point of political debates. The slogan "We are the 99 percent" has entered into the cultural and political lexicon, with some using it as a rallying cry against economic disparity and others calling the concept divisive and un-American.[5]

After the Occupy Wall Street movement created a tent-city in Zuccotti Park, protesters in other cities soon followed its example. Worldwide protests against corporate greed, economic injustice, and political disenfranchisement challenge communities of faith to respond, as the majority of religious people are members of the 99 percent. The Occupy movement rekindles our hope that another world is possible and opens spaces for dialogues and direct actions against the status quo, which benefits a tiny minority. This hope is not the utopian hope of dreamers but finds its roots in grassroots organizing and actions. Young people across the globe have stood up and demanded their voices be heard. In the United States and elsewhere, promising young men and women risk arrest, imprisonment, and death by taking actions to change the world and to create a better future.

The Occupy movement calls for serious reflection on the social and economic teachings of the church, its images of God and other topics, and a public theology that speaks to the challenges of our time. In the 1960s and 1970s, Latin American liberation theology, feminist theology, black theology, and other liberation theologies emerged during the periods of mass social movements against colonialism, economic exploitation, and gender and racial discrimination.[6] Today, some scholars, particularly those residing in North America, argue that these various theological movements are passé and have lost their momentum. No doubt the world has changed, and movements and ways of analyzing the world are changing as well. But much of what liberation theology has to say is still very relevant. The world is in need of liberation more than ever before, and the insistence on the preferential option for the poor is at the heart of many of our most progressive Jewish and Christian traditions. Given the fact that the global economic system has changed dramatically since the 1970s, notions like "the poor," "the oppressed," or "the marginalized" need to be expanded and refined, as economic wealth is increasingly amassed and controlled by a tiny global elite, the so-called 1 percent.[7]

This book is titled *Occupy Religion* because we want to challenge traditional ways of thinking about religion and the space that religion is supposed to inhabit. Since the Enlightenment, many people in the West have espoused the notion that religion should be a private matter, separate from and having little to do with the public sphere. Max Weber has characterized modernity in Western Europe by rationalization and the "disenchantment of the world" at both the personal and societal levels.[8] But in many parts of the world, religion has not stopped exerting enormous influences in public life. Religious fundamentalism has played increasingly important roles in various religions, including the Religious Right in the United States. At the same time, progressive forms of religion have also made a difference. Since September 11, 2001, religion has increasingly entered the public domain in the United States and in policy discussions, especially in the context of terrorism, international relations, and global peace. There has been a notable change of attitude in the secular state and public domain regarding the enduring influences of religion and religious communities.

The term "occupy" has many meanings within the Occupy movement, and there are people who are both for and against the use of this term, as we will discuss in chapter 3. It is not used in a military sense, such as to take hold or take possession of land and property through the use of force or violence. Rather, "occupy" connotes taking back what is supposed to belong to the public, so that power and wealth will be shared more equitably and not concentrated in the hands of a few. It also means creating physical and imaginary spaces so that an alternative world can be thought and experienced. As a verb, "occupy" is action-oriented and means "to employ, busy, or engage (oneself, one's attention, mind, etc.)," according to Webster's New World Dictionary.[9] For the occupiers, this means getting busy and engaging in taking action to change the status quo. In the process, the plight of working people, the poor, and the marginalized has received more attention, combined with a new awareness of the difference that common people can make when they organize.

"Occupy religion" does not mean using force or other means to take over religious institutions and structures, holy sites, worshipping spaces, or religious goods, but rather indicates the conceptualization of a democratic and participatory space for religious life, broadly conceived, and active engagement to make this a reality. It challenges rigid boundaries between the sacred and the profane, as well as between the professional religious elites and the masses, and thus transforms narrow notions of religion as private or otherworldly. "Occupy religion" aims to demystify and debunk religious doctrines and social teachings that provide both religious sanction and justification for economic and social inequality. It critiques religious institutions and structures that silence, discriminate, and marginalize people because of class, race, gender, and sexuality, and thus hand the power to the 1 percent. "Occupy religion" calls religious communities to account and asks them to engage critically in transforming the world to make it just for all and sustainable for the environment.

The concept of "occupy religion" invites us to rethink the nature, purpose, and functions of theology, which means God-talk. For too long, theology has been conceived as a reflection of faith for the internal consumption of religious communities, and as a highly specialized discipline with very abstruse language in the academy. We believe that theology should be done in the public square more intentionally, promoting conversations and stimulating debates for the welfare of the people. Today, we know that theology cannot be separated from life, and that all theology is political, even if it is not aware of this truth.[10] For this reason, theology needs to be more forthcoming in addressing important social and political issues that the public is concerned about and bringing out the public relevance of religious faiths and beliefs. It is interdisciplinary in nature because life cannot be divided up according to disciplines, and it engages the work of critical thinkers, whose ideas and thoughts shape public discourse.

We would like to call the kind of public theology we are proposing "theology of the multitude" inspired by the global mass protests we saw in 2011. The term "multitude" has been popularized by the political theorists Michael Hardt and Antonio Negri. In their influential volume titled *Empire*, they distinguish empire of our time from imperialism of an earlier period because empire "establishes no territorial center of power and does not rely on fixed boundaries and barriers."[11] Imperialism relies on the ruling of foreign territories and peoples by force, by political collaboration, and by economic and cultural dependence. But with the changing role of nation-states and the globalization of capitalist production, the global reach of empire increasingly controls and influences all aspects of our lives. Resisting the forces of empire, a new political subject, which Hardt and Negri call "the multitude," is in the process of rising up. The multitude does not consist of one particular class or sector of society, but includes the working class, migrant and seasonal workers, unpaid domestic laborers, the unemployed and the underemployed, and the poor and the destitute, who also contribute to society. As Hardt and Negri write, "The multitude is thus composed potentially of all the diverse figures of social production."[12] This is what the Occupy movement has called the 99 percent, and it has been joined even by some members of the 1 percent.

The concept of the multitude resonates with the Greek New Testament term *ochlos*, meaning a crowd or mass of people, and the term *laos*, meaning the common people. These terms appear in the Gospels and Acts many times. As we will discuss in more detail in chapter 4, the crowd followed Jesus from place to place as people gathered around him, listened to his parables and teachings, and witnessed his miracles and healing. In the Gospels, the crowd was portrayed as on the side of Jesus and contrasted with the ruling class from Jerusalem. Jesus had "compassion for them, because they were like sheep without a shepherd" (Mark 6:34). A new interpretation of *ochlos* in the

Bible stimulated South Korean theologians to develop what is known as *minjung* theology in the 1970s during their struggles against the dictatorial Park Chung-Hee government. New theological appropriations of *ochlos*, *laos*, or "the multitude" for our time have particular relevance for the Occupy movement today.

Although this book focuses primarily on the Christian tradition, it will also include insights and contributions from other religious traditions. We hope it will stimulate people of other faith communities to think about the meaning of "occupy religion" in their own traditions. Written with general readers in mind, this book is organized along the following lines. Chapter 2 provides the social and economic contexts for the emergence of the Occupy movement and the rhetoric of the 1 percent and the 99 percent. It discusses the shift of geopolitics and implications of the dichotomy of the 1 percent and the 99 percent for religion and everything else in the United States and the world. While most commentators interpret the dichotomy of the 1 percent and the 99 percent strictly in economic terms, we seek to draw out the contrast in broader implications because economic issues can no longer be separated from other aspects of life.

Chapter 3 discusses the Occupy movement within the context of international anti-globalization movements and other grassroots efforts against the exploitation of global capital. It elucidates the concepts of globalization from below and direct democracy, and it shows how they provide important perspectives for looking at the Occupy movement. The Occupy movement has attracted a fair share of criticism as well as support from a wide range of people. The chapter discusses the critics and the cultural brokers and offers examples of how the faith communities have responded to the movement.

In chapter 4, we begin our reflections on a new theology of the multitude. When we bring together the concerns of the 99 percent with concerns raised by various liberative theologies in the recent past, new theological sensitivities emerge. Deep solidarity transforms both the transcendent and the immanent. As a result, the focus shifts from distribution to production. This means that the question is no longer merely whether there is enough to go around (i.e., distribution); the question is also what difference the multitude makes in both church and world (i.e., production).

Fresh visions of the divine are presented in chapter 5. Atheists have a point, we note, because many of the most common images of God resemble the powers that be rather than the liberative manifestations of God that are so deeply embedded in Jewish, Christian, Muslim, and many other religious traditions. Not surprisingly, Christians were considered atheists by the theologians of the Roman Empire. Engaging the divine from the perspective of the 99 percent, we reclaim radical images of God in our traditions that present us with an alternative understanding of power and inspire new relations among people and communities.

Chapter 6 considers the church of the multitude by first discussing how economics and class have affected the development of the structure and life of the church. The Occupy movement stimulates us to think of the *ecclesia* (assembly) of the people of God in new ways, especially in the understanding of sacred space and time. The chapter argues that the church needs to allow the people of God to have a foretaste of God's reign. Through embodying diversity and adopting participatory structures, the church of the multitude can unleash the potential of the people to bear witness to God's shalom.

We believe that a theology of the multitude must be done in consultation with the multitude so that many voices can be heard. In the process of writing this book, we interviewed and spoke to protesters in the Occupy movement and theologians associated with them in New York, Boston, Chicago, Minneapolis, Tucson, Dallas, Lincoln (Nebraska), Oakland, and Los Angeles. We also gathered information from people in other cities when we attended academic and church gatherings in the spring of 2012. In addition, we used a "crowdsourcing" method, soliciting information and comments through Facebook and Twitter, much as the occupiers have done.

As theologians, we have participated in social movements in Asia, Europe, and the United States and have written in various genres related to liberation theology for decades. Kwok Pui-lan grew up in the former British colony of Hong Kong and is involved in the Asian feminist movement. Joerg Rieger grew up in southern Germany and is active in worker justice and other social movements. The collaboration of two persons with different social and cultural backgrounds and worldviews brings novel and complementary perspectives to bear on the subject matter. Kwok, the 2011 president of the American Academy of Religion, is a pioneer of postcolonial theory and cultural studies in religion and theology. Rieger has pioneered a fresh understanding of economics and class in religion and theology as well as empire, and is also conversant with various critical theories. They have worked together before, collaborating with Don H. Compier in editing *Empire and the Christian Tradition: New Readings of Classical Theologians*,[13] which was selected as one of the ten best books in 2008 and won the Best Reference Book of the Year Award in 2008 from the Academy of Parish Clergy.

At a time when many people are puzzled by the Occupy movement and wonder what its future will be, this book provides a helpful guide for Christians and the general public. We hope that these reflections on theology of the multitude will stimulate new theological reflections and perhaps even the emergence of a new theological movement as a response to our time. We offer this book to soulful searchers for justice and to imaginative visionaries whose hearts are prompted by the Spirit. We invite all those who believe in the subversive and transforming power of the God incarnate into the conversation of "occupy religion."

Chapter Two

We Are the 99 Percent

We are the 99 percent. We are getting kicked out of our homes. We are forced
to choose between groceries and rent. We are denied quality medical care. We
are suffering from environmental pollution. We are working long hours for
little pay and no rights, if we're working at all. We are getting nothing while
the other 1 percent is getting everything. We are the 99 percent.
—Tumblr blog of wearethe99percent [1]

The slogan "We are the 99 percent," first blogged and chanted in New York
around mid-September 2011, swiftly became shorthand to describe not only
gross economic disparity in the United States and around the world but also
significant differentials of power that render democracy ineffective. The
Tumblr blog "We Are the 99 Percent" helped popularize the slogan by offering a stark comparison of the 1 percent with the 99 percent. People in the
United States and elsewhere post on the blog personal stories and moving
testimonies of living in anxiety and uncertainty because they have lost their
jobs and are forced to live without health insurance. Others worry about
losing their homes and their savings and belongings to the banks. Younger
people wonder how they can afford to go to college and pay back student
loans. Many express anger and indignation that as hard-working people, they
have no job security, their paychecks are getting smaller, and they are struggling to feed themselves and their families. In the midst of such economic
malaise, the Occupy movement came about and named the source of the
crises of our time: "Wall Street banks, big corporations, and others among
the 1% are claiming the world's wealth for themselves at the expense of the
99% and having their way with our government." [2] It is not difficult to see

why there is such a pervasive outcry that Wall Street and the financial systems it represents need to be occupied. Despite an often-repeated confusion about the Occupy movement by commentators in the press, understanding the movement is not that difficult. Already in October 2011, *Time* magazine had it figured out: "Like the Tea Party . . . their unifying idea is simple enough. The anger they express has a clear target: not the government but the wealthy." In the same article, it was reported that 54 percent of Americans had a favorable view of the Occupy movement, compared to 27 percent who had a favorable view of the Tea Party.[3]

Wall Street, the location of the New York Stock Exchange and other financial institutions, has become a symbol of systemic corporate greed, financial irresponsibility, and gross concentration of wealth. In this view, Wall Street serves the interests of wealthy investors and functions according to the unilateral logic of the 1 percent. This logic assumes that economic growth flows down from top to bottom, benefiting poorer members of the society by improving the economy as a whole in what is called a trickle-down economy. It is most evidently manifested in corporate tax cuts, the reduction of tax rates for capital gains, and government bailouts of banks and financial institutions when they are considered "too big to fail." The logic is backed up by various schools of neoliberal capitalism, which advocates a free market with as little governmental regulation as possible.[4] Economists and other dissenting voices who have questioned the risks and dangers of capitalism run amok are systematically ignored or ridiculed, and risk being labeled socialists.

The Occupy movement protests against this unilateral logic, which has held Wall Street in bondage for over thirty years. This logic has not worked, but rather has harmed and caused hardships for millions of people. On the first day of Occupy Wall Street in New York, more than one thousand people marched from Bowling Green Park amid heavy police presence across the financial district and shouted, "Wall Street is our street," and "Power to the people, not to the banks."[5] A few days later, the General Defense Committee of the Industrial Workers of the World issued a statement supporting Occupy Wall Street, saying, "The only individuals who remain unaffected by the volatility of capitalism, globalization, and the stock market are those who are getting richer from furthering the disparity of all workers through calculated economic calamity."[6] By rallying people from different social and economic sectors, the Occupy movement has ignited a conversation on issues that have not been addressed in the United States in public for a long time, such as income inequality, wealth accumulation, and the concentration of power. In doing so, it has already changed the political discourse. According to a Pew study in December 2011, two-thirds of Americans believed that there were "strong conflicts" between the rich and the poor in the United States, ahead of racial issues and issues of immigration. There was a 59 percent increase compared to a similar survey in 2009, when only 47 percent believed there were strong conflicts between classes.[7]

Yet the neoliberal logic does not govern the economic sphere alone; it increasingly penetrates politics, culture, the media, and even arenas that have been traditionally considered private, such as dating, sex, and religion. The tendrils of the market economy reach deep and wide, not only affecting consumption patterns but also shaping basic values of society, impacting peoples' mindsets and psyches, and transforming the tenor of our relationships. Hannah Hofheinz, a graduate student from Harvard, says, "I am occupied," when referring to her school as a place that reproduces the 1 percent.[8] During a protest of the Dallas Occupy movement in front of a Bank of America building, artist Goran Maric noted the narrowing of the public space in which the 99 percent can operate. Perched between a busy street and the Bank of America property, to which access was restricted, Maric pointed to the narrow sidewalk on which the protestors gathered and stated, "This is the width of our freedom." The Occupy movement is a wake-up call to rethink how Wall Street and runaway capitalism have shaped and changed our everyday life. The question before all of us is whether our work, our actions, and even our religions support the 1 percent or the alternative visions of the 99 percent.

THE 1 PERCENT AND THE 99 PERCENT

The Occupy movement has succeeded in bringing into American public conversation the idea that there is a fundamental dichotomy between the 1 percent and the 99 percent. While there are other insights and demands of the Occupy movement that are worthy of discussion, the dichotomy between the 1 percent and the 99 percent colors everything else. For the most part, in the United States we have thought of ourselves as a society in which class does not matter. And even when we have talked about underprivileged groups, such as the poor or the homeless, we have not emphasized underlying class dichotomies that shape so much of our reality. On those occasions when class is brought up—for instance, when discussing social stratification, a topic that is more acceptable to talk about in the United States—people often display a regrettable lack of understanding of class dichotomy.[9] Some progressives have even suggested moving away from the term "class" because of what they see as the "negative connotations" of the term "lower class." Yet it is doubtful that merely renaming a reality without changing it will lead to results.

At first sight, proclaiming a dichotomy between the 1 percent and the 99 percent might seem overly simplistic and perhaps even naive. But even Joseph E. Stiglitz of Columbia University, a former chief economist of the World Bank and Nobel laureate in economics, refers to income inequality in the United States as the wealthy 1 percent versus the remaining 99 percent. He states, "Of all the costs imposed on our society by the top 1 percent, perhaps the greatest is this: the erosion of our sense of identity, in which fair play, equality of opportunity, and a sense of community are so important."[10] The sheer numbers behind the dichotomy between the 1 percent and the 99 percent are staggering: the members of the top 1 percent now own more than half of the wealth in the United States and, more important, this wealth allows them to wield incredible power. To be even more specific, in the United States, four hundred individuals have more wealth than 60 percent of all Americans.[11] Wealth distribution has changed dramatically in the past decades. While in 1962 the wealthiest 1 percent of households averaged 125 times the wealth of the median household, in 2009 the wealthiest 1 percent of households averaged 225 times the wealth of the median household.[12] Jared Bernstein of the Center on Budget and Policy Priorities reports, "Between 1979 and 2007, incomes grew by 275 percent for the wealthiest 1 percent of households, 37 percent for the middle 60 percent of households, and 18 percent for the poorest 20 percent of households."[13]

In the first decade of the twenty-first century, which began with the climax of the dot.com boom and subsequent bust and ended with the Great Recession, middle-class income took a steep hit, falling by 7 percent from $53,164 in 2000 to $49,445 in 2010, when adjusted for inflation. The U.S. Census Bureau reported that the poverty rate rose to a seventeen-year high. As many as 46.2 million people (or 15.1 percent of the U.S. population) live in poverty and 49.9 million live without health insurance.[14] Forty-five thousand people in the United States die each year because they do not have health insurance, hundreds of thousands have no choice but to suffer without health care, and four million are losing their homes.[15] Furthermore, the wealth gaps between the different races have grown to their widest levels since the government began tabulating them a quarter-century ago. The recession and uneven economic recovery have erased decades of minority gains. New census data shows that the net worth of white people, on average, is twenty times that of blacks, and eighteen times that of Hispanics.[16] According to a study by the National Urban League, the black middle class has lost all the ground that was gained in the past thirty years, as black unemployment has risen to levels comparable to 1982, and as high as 20 percent.[17] At the same time, all economic gains in 2012, as of this writing, were pocketed by the 1 percent; no one else saw any increase.[18]

The United States is more divided by class than any other advanced industrialized country. The level of income inequality in the United States is comparable to levels in countries such as Cameroon, Madagascar, Rwanda, Uganda, and Ecuador—not a very flattering picture. Even China, where a severe income gap has been a source of worsening political instability, has a more equal income distribution than that of the United States.[19] As a result of this gross inequality, the often-invoked notion of class struggle is an everyday reality, although it is waged primarily from the top down rather than from the bottom up: the loss of jobs and income for the 99 percent is no accident, as it happens precisely at the same time that the fortunes of the 1 percent are increasing substantially. Even the cuts in benefits and health care for the 99 percent are matched by an increase in benefits packages—including substantial severance pay—for the elites. This sort of class struggle is what has created and exacerbated the dichotomy between the 1 percent and the 99 percent. When the 1 percent have consistently gained even in times of economic crisis, while the 99 percent are gaining less and less even in times of economic progress, the argument that a rising tide will lift all boats rings increasingly hollow.[20] A record 48 percent of all Americans are now considered low income.[21]

When we talk about the dichotomy between the 1 percent and the 99 percent, we are talking about a relationship. This relationship is marked by both differentials of money and, perhaps more importantly, differentials of power. The notion of class can help us think about these kinds of relationships. It will also enable us to think more clearly about questions such as "Who wins and who loses?" and "Who is in control and who is not?" We raise these questions not merely to understand what is going on, but also to find out what the possible alternatives might be. A deeper understanding of class, which is to say a deeper understanding of how we are related to each other, might also help us avoid another danger, which has to do with moralizing these topics.

We wish to emphasize that the purpose of addressing the notion of class is not to demonize anyone, but quite the opposite. If we begin to understand that the challenge we are facing has to do with structural class relationships, we will stop demonizing individuals. The inherent problem of the dichotomy of the 1 percent and the 99 percent is not primarily the greed of individual CEOs or bankers, as many have assumed. On the contrary, the problem is precisely that CEOs or bankers as individuals have relatively few choices in the neoliberal and transnational economy in which they find themselves. When this fact becomes clear, it helps us understand why even individual members of the 1 percent occasionally join in with the 99 percent and support their concerns. The 1 percent are not excluded from the Occupy movement but are invited to make their own contributions to the well-being of all. In fact, a small movement of the 1 percent supporting the 99 percent is already under way.[22] Even billionaire investors like Warren Buffett and George Soros have publicly supported the proposal to increase taxes on the wealthy. Soros went on record stating that if there is a "better distribution of income, the average American will be better off."[23]

The big news when talking about class is that 99 percent of the population find themselves to be in the same boat and suffer to some degree from similar unjust economic and financial systems. While there are, of course, significant differences within the 99 percent, what we have in common is that the economy is working less and less to our benefit and that our voices matter less and less in all areas of life. This insight is especially important for those of us who have traditionally considered ourselves middle class. Our current economic and political reality shows that there is no safe place in the middle. While the economy goes up and down in cycles, and the fortunes of the 1 percent recover when the market rises, the fortunes of more and more people do not. Even in the most devastating economic crisis since the Great Depression, a few people have gained while almost everybody else has lost. These losses can be expressed in terms of people's net worth, retirement accounts, and salaries and benefits. But the most important losses are associated with the decrease of power in the workplace and in other public arenas.

The precarious situation of the American working class offers a lens to look at the predicament of the 99 percent. The American working class has seen their income falling and their bargaining power eroded. In the current economic climate, workers are often treated as disposable and expendable, which exposes the enormous gap between their interests and the interests of big businesses. The corporate laws in the United States protect the interests of the stockholders but not those of the workers. The CEOs of corporations are accountable to their stockholders and work for their interests and benefits. Dominant stockholders have successfully sued CEOs, beginning with Henry Ford, if they showed too much concern for their workers.[24]

At the most basic level, this dichotomy between CEOs and workers is shown in their income differentials. The average CEO in the United States makes 350 times more than the average worker, up from 50 times during 1960–1985. While corporate profits have doubled since 1990, the average "production worker" pay has increased only by 4 percent. After adjusting for inflation, average hourly earnings have not increased in fifty years, and the minimum wage has dropped.[25] The separation of the CEOs and the workers can also be seen in the level of power the CEOs wield in determining working conditions, promotion and retention, and corporate policies. Another number is perhaps even more telling: top investors—many of them CEOs— earn as much as twenty thousand times what average workers earn.[26] Because of their wealth, the CEOs and investors can lobby local and federal governments and officials for legislation to protect and advance their own and their companies' interests.

The condition of the American working class sheds light on the dichotomy between the 1 percent and the 99 percent in the global context. Considering the subject of class from the perspective of financial stratification, some have argued that all the inhabitants of the so-called First World belong to the 1 percent when compared to people in the rest of the world. It is certainly important to remember the disparity of incomes and living standards of people living in different countries and regions of the world. But such simple generalization leaves out many details and overlooks the fact that class is not just a matter of money but also one of power and relationships. Members of the working class in the United States may own a house and a car, but they have fairly limited power, and the little power they have has been undermined by concerted attacks on unions and other organizations representing their interests. Membership in labor unions has dropped precipitously in the United States. In the 1950s, 36 percent of the workers were unionized; in 2008, only 12.4 percent of wage and salary workers were union members.[27] Workers in some countries in Latin America, on the contrary, may be better organized in trade unions and may enjoy more rights.

In addition, workers in the United States and workers in the so-called Third World are controlled by the same transnational capitalist class, which we will discuss further below. There are parallels in the exploitation of work, as well as in being expendable. According to one estimate, as much as 23 percent of the workforce in the United States was unemployed at the end of 2011.[28] The income differential between CEOs and workers in the United States is far greater than the income differential between the working class in the United States and in the so-called Third World, including the casually employed. In addition, the wealthy 1 percent exists not only in the United States but also elsewhere. After all, the richest person in the world is Mexican billionaire Carlos Slim Helú.

In the past, we members of the American middle class have often felt that we were benefiting from the wealth and the power of the 1 percent. Even if we have not consciously reflected on it, we have considered ourselves to be in closer proximity to the ruling class than to the working class. Many of us have intuitively agreed with the often-repeated but never proven mantra of neoliberal capitalism that a rising tide will lift all boats. But the reality is that the fate of the middle class resembles more and more the fate of the working class: our savings and stockholdings are getting smaller and smaller, our jobs are less secure, and our influence is declining.[29] The economic downturn and the tightening of state budgets have led to massive layoffs of teachers and other professionals in the public and private sectors. Many middle-class families find that they are only one or two paychecks away from poverty. Older professionals and skilled workers often find themselves hitting a brick wall when they try to get back into the labor market after being laid off.

This opens the door for what we are calling deep solidarity.[30] Whereas solidarity in the past for the middle class has often meant deciding to side with those less fortunate than us, we are beginning to understand that solidarity cuts deeper than this. Rather than trying to understand the condition of those less fortunate in terms of our own, we are beginning to see ourselves in terms of those we have considered less fortunate. Without glossing over the differences, we begin to see their fate as our fate. We are also the 99 percent.

NOBODY WINS UNLESS EVERYBODY WINS

From the very beginning, the concerns of the Occupy movement were not limited to justice for Americans, but rather included justice for the whole human family. Some of the early organizers of Occupy Wall Street participated in the protests in Europe and they clearly saw the connections of the Occupy movement with the uprisings in Europe and the Middle East. One of the organizers expressed this broader concern in this way: "The people are not here for the American economic crisis. They're here for the crisis of the world."[31] An early declaration of the General Assembly of Occupy Wall Street also states:

> As one people, united, we acknowledge the reality: that the future of the human race requires the cooperation of its members; that our system must protect our rights, and upon corruptions of that system, it is up to the individuals to protect their own rights, and those of their neighbors.[32]

The plight of the 99 percent of the world is closely connected due to an economic system that is marked by the rapid flow of capital and raw materials and by the exploitation of labor, which knows fewer and fewer national or geographical boundaries.

In response to these pressures, the Occupy movement went global on October 15, 2011, when demonstrators in 952 cities in eighty-two countries marched under "October 15" banners or the hashtag "#GlobalChange." They protested against income inequality as well as exploitation of one class by another; the corruption of officials as well as systems that breed corruption; the pollution of the environment, which affects the lower classes most of all; gross violations of human rights; and other social problems specific to their contexts. The protesters were clear that these are not minor grievances or imperfections of a system that otherwise functions well, but matters of life and death for humanity and the planet. Another global protest was planned for the spring of 2012. People from the Spanish *Indignados* and Occupy movements from across the world called for a Global Spring, beginning in May, with a catchy slogan: "Nobody wins unless everybody wins."[33]

In today's globalizing economy, things are changing rapidly. The nineteenth-century Marxist analysis, for instance, which states that the capitalist class is organized in terms of nation-states and driven by national capitalist competition and rivalries between nations, has to be modified and updated. We have to look beyond the international system of states to understand how the world has changed since the last decades of the twentieth century. What has emerged is a transnational capitalist class that has the power to control production and accumulation beyond national borders and economies. This class is at the top of the 1 percent, and since "class" is a relational term, it is important to understand its dynamics in order to understand the place of the 99 percent. William I. Robinson and Jerry Harris define the transnational capitalist class as "that segment of the world bourgeoisie that represents transnational capital, the owners of the leading worldwide means of production as embodied in the transnational corporations and private financial institutions."[34] This new class has become a global system in which Japanese capitalists are as comfortable investing in Latin America as American capitalists are in Southeast Asia. The development of global and interconnected businesses and industries makes this new class the driver of world capitalism. The nation-states have not disappeared but are serving these developments and supporting them through their power, including their military force.[35]

Transnational capitalist class formation is a key aspect of the globalization process, which has changed the circuits of capital and dramatically restructured the relationships of production that affect the lives of the 99 percent. Hedge-fund managers and investment bankers serve an international clientele made up of members of the 1 percent, helping them to transfer capital and wealth at lightning speed. There has been a sharp increase in direct foreign investments. Such investments are no longer unilaterally from the Global North to the Global South, as businesses and entrepreneurs from emerging markets—Brazil, Russia, India, and China—look for opportunities to maximize their profits. Transnational business partnerships are formed to compete for huge global projects, and mergers and acquisitions occur across national borders.

It is the globalization of production that provides the base of the transnational capital class. Much was written in the 1970s and 1980s about exploitation by transnational corporations, such as the use of cheap labor and pollution of the environment. Since then, globalization of production has intensified, which entails the fragmentation of production into many steps and segments and dispersing them worldwide according to labor cost and a range of other considerations that allow maximizing profit opportunities. The production system is no longer located in one country, but fragmented in different locales and tightly integrated into new globalized circuits of capital accumulation. As such, this worldwide decentralization of the production process is taking place under the centralization of control of the global economy by transnational capital.

Take, for example, the production of popular Apple products such as iPhones and iPads. Apple employs 43,000 people in the United States and 20,000 overseas. But an additional 700,000 work for Apple's contractors overseas, which build and assemble iPhones, iPads, and Apple's other products. The iPhones contain hundred of parts, and an estimated 90 percent of the parts are manufactured abroad. As the *New York Times* reports, "Advanced semiconductors have come from Germany and Taiwan, memory from Korea and Japan, display panels and circuitry from Korea and Taiwan, chipsets from Europe and rare metals from Africa and Asia. And all of it is put together in China."[36] Apple products are assembled and manufactured by Foxconn, a multinational electronics manufacturing company headquartered in Taiwan, which has dozens of facilities in Asia, Eastern Europe, Mexico, and Brazil. Foxconn assembles nearly 40 percent of the world's consumer electronics products and serves Apple, Amazon, Dell, Hewlett-Packard, Motorola, Nintendo, Nokia, Samsung, and Sony.

Many Americans ask why companies such as Apple have to offshore their production overseas and not employ American workers, when so many cannot find work. Even President Barack Obama asked, "What would it take to make iPhones in the United States?" when he visited California in 2011 and dined with Silicon Valley's top luminaries. A closer look at the huge Foxconn City in Shenzhen, China, provides some clues. The facility employs 230,000 workers, many of whom work six days a week, often spending twelve hours in the plant. While some workers live in surrounding villages and towns, about one-quarter live in factory dormitories. Many of them earn less than $17 a day. They work overtime and under pressure when production demands. The scale of the facility and the regimentation of the workforce are hardly imaginable in the United States. Apple has been the target of criticism following reports of accidents and suicides at the Foxconn site. Labor rights groups report that eighteen Chinese workers at Foxconn killed themselves, or tried to, in 2010. The incidents brought international attention to the exploitation of Chinese workers by foreign companies, which demand their workers to work like machines and pay no attention to the human cost.[37]

Globalization and "race to the bottom" strategies adopted by the transnational capitalist class require a steady supply of cheap and flexible labor. Women in developing countries provide a huge pool of cheap labor for

capitalist production. Sociologist Saskia Sassen has studied the systemic relation between globalization and the feminization of wage labor. She points
out that immigration and offshore production have evolved into mechanisms
for the massive incorporation of women in developing countries into wage
labor. As in the case of Foxconn, many young women are recruited to work
in transnational companies in new industrial zones throughout the world.
Many of these women migrate from rural areas with few skills and little work
experience. They concentrate in export manufacturing of electronics, gar-
ments, textiles, and toys. They are employed in low-wage jobs where workers' empowerment is almost nonexistent. During economic downturns and
times when changes in demands occur, they are often the first ones to get laid
off. The female migrant workers are characterized by a double disadvantage:
gender and class.[38]

In a world restructured by the transnational capitalist class, many men and
women compete to work in these transnational factories and manufacturing
plants in order to leave their rural villages and go to the cities to find a better
life for themselves and their families. To be exploited by the global manufacturing powerhouses would even seem to be a privilege. Others who are
excluded from any meaningful participation in the global economy, including the poor and vulnerable, peasants, and millions of women and children,
are left scrambling to live. As the transnational capitalist class amasses profits and wealth, the unjust world economy leaves 2.7 billion people to survive
on US$2 per day or less, a condition that contributes to social unrest, ethnic
strife, and (in some cases) prolonged civil wars. This global situation affects
the 99 percent in the United States more directly than is commonly realized,
as workers are pitted against workers around the globe, increasingly affecting
even middle-class jobs that once felt secure. More than 50 percent of the
better jobs that were lost during the economic crisis in the United States are
never going to come back.[39]

Puleng LenkaBula from South Africa argues that the neoliberal market
logic has forced African countries to open their national boundaries and
resources, adopt stringent structural adjustments, and privatize state-owned
enterprises. Increasingly, basic services and goods, such as water, pensions,
and health care, have been contracted out to private businesses. In these
cases, the role of the state in both regulating business practices and providing
public services has been reduced due to the pressures imposed by global
financial institutions and transnational capital. At the same time, the role of
the state is useful to business when it imposes austerity measures. Although

foreign investments are sorely needed for the poor countries in Africa, investors reap enormous profits and can easily move their capital out, without much benefit to the people who work for them.[40] The problems faced by the African nations can be seen also in other nations of the world because they, too, are under the pressures of the same global economic system.

In order to keep its profits growing, the transnational capitalist class needs to control labor and production and ensure a steady supply of valuable natural resources. If necessary, military power has to be deployed to protect their vested interests and exert control. As Douglas Keller argues, the foreign policy of President George W. Bush exhibited a "militarism in which US military power is used to advance US interests and geopolitical hegemony."[41] This policy, he says, was first evident in the intervention in Afghanistan following the events of September 11, 2001, and became crystal clear in the preemptive strikes and invasion of Iraq, using as its excuse the assertion that Saddam Hussein was developing weapons of mass destruction. But these weapons were nowhere to be found. The beneficiaries in Iraq in particular were U.S. business interests, who in the wake of the war were able to expand their control of parts of the Persian Gulf and its vast oil reserves.

Safeguarding access to oil production is crucial not only for the dominance of U.S. business interests but also for business interests in emerging global powers, especially China—the world's second-largest economy. A new model of state capitalism has been developed in countries such as Russia and China, with tight connections between the government and businesses, whose main agents come from the 1 percent. For its economic expansion and continued growth, China's 1 percent is interested in building a Eurasian railway network connecting Central Asia through the Middle East and as far as Europe to transport people and resources faster across this vast region. In order to ensure access to Middle Eastern oil, China has strengthened ties with Syria, Turkey, and Iran.[42] China's growing economic power and its competition with the United States for global leadership has increased the military significance of the Pacific for American hegemony.

Big corporations and transnational capital want to control oil, as well as basic necessities such as food and water through patenting of seeds, speculating on food prices, controlling ecosystems, and privatizing and enclosing water commons. Record high prices for staple foods in 2011 were among the contributing causes of the Arab Spring uprisings in Africa and the Middle East, as well as bread riots in other parts of the world. Fears of hunger and famine lead to social unrest, intensify ethnic conflicts, and unravel the social fabric. In addition, water wars have been waged for years in countries in Africa and the Middle East. Tunisia, Algeria, Libya, Yemen, and Bahrain, countries where the Arab uprisings took place, are among the world's most water-scarce countries as a result of population pressure and other environmental factors.

By addressing the disparities of the global economy that benefit primarily the big banks and corporations, the Occupy movement exposes the flawed logic of the transnational capitalist class—the 1 percent—and rallies the world's 99 percent. One of the slogans captures the outrage: "Banks got bailed out! We got sold out!" Participants in the movement marched with banners and held up signs such as "Occupy together," "The rich cannot have everything," "Money talks, 99 percent walks," and "The 99% will not be silent." When interviewed by *Time*, the Indian social activist Aruna Roy clearly articulated the links between the Occupy protests in the advanced capitalist world and anticorruption protests in India and Brazil and the Arab Spring uprisings against dictatorial regimes:

> The "divine force" of market globalization has clearly benefited a few but has failed to positively affect the lives of many. The globalization of dissent has brought together an otherwise disunited and disparate majority against the centers of global finance. The Occupy protests are significant because they bring attention to the unaccountable power of global finance and markets, which are loyal only to their financial masters. [43]

WHAT ARE THE ALTERNATIVES?

The Occupy movement has helped us develop a clearer sense of what we are up against not only in economics and politics but in all other areas of life as well, thus broadening our horizons so that we can envision new alternatives. Sensing that something is not right, many Americans have taken to criticizing the government. When something goes wrong in the economy, the government gets the blame. But if government control is the root of all evil, as many Americans believe, why has the influence of the 1 percent over the government so rarely been addressed? While there are indeed problems with American democracy and the role of the government, the Occupy movement reminds us that we can only get to the bottom of these problems if we consider the power of the 1 percent, which greatly influences political processes without public mandate. While government officials are at least elected and vetted to some degree by the public, members of the 1 percent have no obligation to be accountable to the public. The Supreme Court's decision that the government may not ban political spending by corporations on elections and campaigns gives the 1 percent heightened influence on the political process, but this is only the tip of the iceberg. Yet such rulings further add fuel to the public cynicism that elections can be bought and the government cannot be trusted.

While some Americans criticize the government, others blame the decline of social morality, the breakdown of families, and cultural malaise for problems Americans face. Consumer culture, in particular, is frequently lifted up as a problem. The solution they offer is to adopt a countercultural stance, which often has a conservative bent. What is overlooked is the fact that culture, and the culture of consumerism in particular, is often shaped by the interests of powerful elites. Without this awareness, a countercultural stance does not go deep enough because it ends up opposing the wrong people. The globalization of the capitalist system reproduces itself by maintaining consumerism—for which the consumers themselves are often blamed. Leslie Sklair writes, "Global capitalism thrives by persuading us that the meaning and value of our lives are to be found principally in what we possess, that we can never be totally satisfied with our possessions."[44] Much of the desire that drives consumerism is not a natural human instinct, but has to be produced and reproduced through advertisements and the media.[45] So while there are certainly problems with American culture, the Occupy movement points out that there are hidden interests driving our culture, which are linked not to the interests of the 99 percent but to those of the 1 percent. Without this deeper analysis, becoming countercultural gets stuck on the surface, blaming the victims and failing to address the deeper problems.

Still others blame religion as the root and the core of all deception. The so-called neo-atheists, such as Richard Dawkins, Sam Harris, and Christopher Hitchens, are anti-religious activists who attack belief in God and accuse religion of indoctrinating people and misleading them. Yet religion as such may not be the problem either. While religion has certainly been used and shaped very often by the forces of empire and in the interests of the ruling classes, there are also examples of religion joining the resistance and providing alternatives. Throughout the history of the United States, for instance, religion has been deeply involved with progressive movements, such as the abolitionist movement, the suffragist movement, the civil rights movement, the peace movement, and the labor movement.

The Occupy movement's focus on the differential between the 1 percent and the 99 percent sheds new light on the phenomenon of religion. Similar to politics and culture, religion also needs to be seen in the context of the dichotomy between the 1 percent and the 99 percent. The power of the 1 percent extends to religion as well, and so it is not surprising that even in the world of religious praxis, there are growing efforts to organize religious communities like corporations. The megachurches are often used as examples of this trend, but the recent reorganizations of many United Methodist Annual Conferences in the United States in ways that centralize decision-making and limit established democratic structures point in the same direction. Theology has, in many cases, provided support for these efforts—for instance, when the idea of the Lordship of Jesus Christ is couched in terms of the power of a CEO.[46] And even if Jesus's Lordship is not explicitly reshaped in terms of the interests of the 1 percent, there is little theological reflection in mainline white churches on how the Lordship of Jesus Christ might support alternative power in both church and world.[47]

We talk about "occupy religion" because we are convinced that religious communities and institutions can be forces to serve justice and the common good. There is a deep concern in our religious traditions for just relationships and the flourishing of all, in particular the "least of these" (Matt. 25:45). The religious logic that we will develop in this book tells us that only if they can live well can we all live well, and if they perish, we all perish.

At the same time, we talk about "occupy religion" in ways that resemble what was called *Kirchenkampf* (church struggle) in Nazi Germany. This struggle of the churches was not one of church against state, although the term is often misunderstood in this way, but rather of the church that supported the fascist status quo against alternative forms of the church, which resisted the powers that be. The ultimate goal was *Gleichschaltung* (bringing into line), the assimilation of alternative religion to the interests of the status quo. At a time when religion is once again more and more identified with the status quo, at stake is nothing less than the future of religion itself. As we study and examine distorted forms of the religion of the status quo, we need to ask deeper questions as to the causes of these distortions. Where can we find idol worship and idolatry, and what drives them?[48] How is religion affected by the tensions between the 1 percent and the 99 percent? Recall that in the biblical narratives of the Exodus, idols were never mere religious symbols but rather tied to interests of power. The golden calf, for instance, was both an idol and an expression of wealth and power that rivaled the power of the liberating divinity of the Exodus (Exod. 32).

As we begin to understand what we are up against in terms of the dichotomy between the 1 percent and the 99 percent, we are not proposing to instigate class warfare. This is, of course, one of the most popular accusations against the Occupy movement in the United States. But what this accusation overlooks is that class warfare has been waged for a long time, mostly from the top down, against both workers and the middle class. Today we see such class warfare, for instance, when the right of American workers to unionize is challenged more strongly in the United States than in most other capitalist economies, or when the employed and the unemployed are intentionally pitted against each other in order to maximize the profit of corporations. We also see class warfare in the discussion of taxes, as any reduction of the tax burdens of the wealthiest individuals and corporations implies significant additional burdens for the rest of society—that is, for the 99 percent.

Understanding what we are up against is the first step, for our goal is to be able to develop alternatives. The Occupy movement embodies some of these alternatives, however imperfect. Perhaps the most important issue of all is that the emerging power of the 99 percent does not seek to duplicate the top-down power of the 1 percent. In addition, the emerging unity of the 99 percent differs from the unity of the 1 percent. This has implications for how we think about solidarity as well.

The unity of the 1 percent might be described in terms of uniformity. It is the uniformity of economic theory (like the belief that a rising tide lifts all boats), the uniformity of politics (like the single-issue politics of tax cuts for the wealthy), and the uniformity of religion (like the idea of God as unilaterally controlling top-down power). While there are a few members of the 1 percent who disagree and put themselves on the side of the 99 percent, solidarity in this context for the most part means supporting others who are like oneself and signing on to a particular creed that is very narrow when it comes to the question of power—namely, that power always flows from the top down, and only top-down power is considered worthy of support.

The unity of the 99 percent, by contrast, can only be unity in diversity. Uniformity is not an option. In terms of economic theory, the unity of the 99 percent is the acknowledgment of the existence of a variety of people-centered economic theories. In terms of politics, it is the acknowledgment of more substantial forms of democracy that cherish the voice and the agency of the people; in terms of religion, it is the acknowledgment of a multiplicity of popular traditions that preach not only concern for the least of these but also a reversal and broadening of power, which moves from the bottom up, so that all can participate in the production of life. The traditions of the prophets in the Hebrew Bible and of Jesus in the Gospels exemplify such popular traditions and such a reversal and broadening of power. Solidarity in this context is not the support of people who are exactly like oneself but rather what we are calling deep solidarity. Solidarity is the support of others who are different yet experience similar predicaments.

The power of the 1 percent is a sort of unilateral power. It is the power that moves from the top down, from one to the many. In the boardrooms of corporations, for instance, CEOs make their decisions considering the interests of the major stockholders, and they are supported by executive boards that they themselves have often invited or appointed. In politics, the power of the 1 percent is readily visible in campaign financing and the host of lobbyists that congregate in Washington, DC. This is, of course, merely the tip of the iceberg, as the influence of money in politics goes much deeper. In religion, the unilateral power of the 1 percent can be seen in structures that show no respect for the concerns of the people. This is not just a problem of some classical and hierarchical traditions, such as the Roman Catholic Church; it is also a common mode of operation in those contemporary church formations that mimic corporations.

The power of the 99 percent, by contrast, is diversified power. One of the most interesting and controversial features of the Occupy movement is that it has not been driven by a small number of easily identifiable leading figures. This is not a weakness, but rather a strength, which has a lot to do with alternative forms of power. In economics, providing room for the diversified power of all that are involved in production is a new model, and it has produced some success in various contexts.[49] In politics, power is based on the concerns of the community. The Occupy movement has practiced this power very intentionally. For instance, people can express themselves in the general assemblies, and decisions are made using the consensus model of participatory democracy. One of the challenges of the Occupy movement is that many of its participants are white and belong to the middle class. This issue will have to be addressed, yet the notion that the Occupy movement is all white is a myth. Members from many diverse groups have been part of it, including a prominent group of African American pastors. The Rev. Graylan

S. Hagler, of Plymouth Congregational United Church of Christ in Northeast Washington, DC, stated, "This is the continuation of the [civil rights] movement. It was the economic movement that King was killed for."[50]

What would the diversified power of the 99 percent look like in religion? A time-honored model can be found in the Latin American base Christian communities, where people refused to support the status quo religion and began to read the Bible together in the context of their everyday struggles. These communities found all over Latin America include people from all walks of life, and when they read the Bible there are no privileged interpreters, despite the fact that trained theologians are often part of these groups. In the context of the Occupy movement, religious faith and spirituality have also played certain roles. Members of the clergy, seminarians, and other spiritual leaders have been involved as protest chaplains, workshops have been conducted on religious topics, and books on religion have found their ways into the libraries of the movements.[51] Yet religion does not seek to dominate; instead, it becomes part of the larger quest for liberation. As such, it can find its own voice and contribute its distinct insights without falling into the trap of exercising control like the 1 percent.

People have often asked whether religious communities and people of faiths should take sides when discussing the Occupy movement. It is important to emphasize that those who think they are not taking sides have already taken a side. In situations of great power imbalance, even those who choose to stay neutral and objective become part of the problem. This is one of the important lessons of the Christian churches in Nazi Germany, where we learned in hindsight that the declared neutrality of some churches actually supported the status quo. This is one of the lessons we have to learn again today. Nevertheless, nothing is ever predetermined. Even members of the 1 percent can choose to join the 99 percent.

The bigger question, however, has to do with the 99 percent: Will they understand what side they are on and shape their thinking and their lives accordingly, or will they continue with business as usual, which tends to support the interests of the 1 percent? The question of class presents us with these issues in a new way, demanding that we reflect on old religious and political traditions, including the self-understanding of the early American leaders when they wrote and adopted "We, the People."

One of the major lessons of the Occupy movement for the study and practice of religion is that our work, if it is to provide genuine alternatives, can no longer be done in isolation. For the study of religion, this means we need to understand how our work and cultural productions are shaped by the scholarly community and contribute to it, as well as how they are influenced by the larger tectonics of power shaping religion, politics, and economics. In other words, our work is shaped in the dynamics of the tensions between the 1 percent and the 99 percent, and affects and contributes to this tension in one way or another. For the practice of religion, this means that we need to understand how religious communities are embedded in this larger context and what differences they can make. The question, first and foremost, is not what religious communities should or ought to do, but rather what is happening and what the viable alternatives are, based on careful analyses and praxis in real life.

In conclusion, the understanding that, unless we take a side, our side will be chosen for us creates new forms of unity and solidarity. We have not seen such unity and solidarity in a long time, as unity and solidarity are usually produced by the status quo, which assumes that we are all the same. Yet if it makes any sense to talk about the unity of the 99 percent, it can only be unity in diversity. Rather than trying to re-create the unity of the 1 percent, the 99 percent only becomes stronger when they respect the diversities in their midst, in terms of race, ethnicity, gender, sexuality, and other markers of differences. This is the deep solidarity we want to suggest. Understanding that we are all in the same boat, it is imperative that we take each other more seriously in our differences while working together on alternatives that provide life for everybody.

Chapter Three

The Multitude Springs into Action

> "99 to 1. Those are great odds. Stand together."
> "Lost a job, found an occupation."
> "When injustice becomes law, resistance becomes duty."
> "This is not a protest. This is a process."
> "This revolution will not be privatized."
> —Posters of the Occupy movement

Brendan Curran, a seminarian in his twenties, participated in Occupy Boston from the beginning. He recalled, "It astonished me when I got to the Boston Common, and witnessed thousands of people waving red and black flags, carrying signs that called for class struggle, and heard the chant 'We are the 99 percent' bouncing off the walls of the statehouse and the surrounding buildings."[1] The crowd consisted of college and graduate students, activists, homeless people, and young professionals. After a campsite was established in Dewey Square in the financial district, Curran slept occasionally in one of tents. He later said, "Rather than merely protesting by having some scheduled and permitted parade I was amazed to see camps spring up like miniature autonomous zones in every major city. I watched people try to experiment and model different modes of organization and a collective effort be made to manifest a more cooperative and compassionate way of being." For his generation, this was something that they had not seen before.

The Occupy movement captured the imagination of many young people in the United States and around the world. Some of them, like Curran, had participated in various kinds of social protests and movements before. Others were holding protest signs for the first time to denounce an economic system that they think is fundamentally unjust. Many of them belong to the Millennial generation or the Net generation, born from the late 1970s to the late 1990s. They are globally aware, since they have grown up with technologies such as the World Wide Web, text messaging, MP3, and social networks. Many carry smart phones and other mobile devices that give them up-to-date information on what is happening in the world and connect them instantaneously with people around the globe.

In addition to young people, the Occupy movement attracted people from across diverse sectors and strata of society. Unlike conventional political activism, the Occupy movement does not have an easily identifiable set of goals and the demands, strategies, and tactics to achieve them. Instead, it represents the coming together of the multitude to express their political will and to develop a process so that people with many diverse interests and agendas can learn to work together to bring about social change. Gary Dorrien, a social ethicist at the Union Theological Seminary in New York, has observed, "They are building a social movement that prizes radical democracy, radical hospitality, and a distinct blend of nonviolence and outrage."[2] These qualities are applied not only to the world of politics but also to the world of economics and to the transformation of everyday relationships, including religion.

The multitude is not a crowd of people without purpose. In this book, the multitude is understood as a political subject with social consciousness that has the power to shape its destiny and change the world. The multitude is a political project in the making that is formed through specific practices and concrete actions. Michael Hardt and Antonio Negri write, "The multitude is not a spontaneous political subject but a project of political organization."[3] We agree with Hardt and Negri's attempts to shift the emphasis from "being the multitude" to "making the multitude." The multitude in many parts of the world has risen up again and again to call attention to exploitation by transnational corporations, unequal trade agreements, unfair labor conditions, destruction of the livelihood of small farmers and poor people, governments that work for the highest bidder, a lack of democratic decision-making, and suppression of political dissent. The Occupy movement offers us a concrete example of the formation of a global multitude and its organization to form a positive political force.

GLOBALIZATION FROM BELOW

Since the end of the Cold War and the disintegration of the Soviet Union and the Eastern Bloc, many politicians, academics, and commentators have declared the triumph of capitalism and liberal democracy over communism. In *The End of History and the Last Man*, Francis Fukuyama argues that the advent of Western liberal democracy might signal the endpoint of humanity's ideological evolution and the final form of government.[4] Many continue to believe that the only way poor countries can lift themselves out of poverty is to transition into a market economy and join the globalizing free-trade system. Unfortunately, the neoliberal economy that has been enforced for over three decades and ruled supreme since the 1990s has not resulted in a better world. In fact, the opposite is the case, as it has allowed wealth to concentrate increasingly in the hands of the 1 percent.

As chief economist of the World Bank, Joseph E. Stiglitz visited many countries and observed globalization at work firsthand. In *Globalization and Its Discontents*, he concludes, "Globalization today is not working for many of the world's poor. It is not working for much of the environment. It is not working for the stability of the global economy."[5] Today, it is becoming clearer that globalization is not even working for the middle class anymore, creating a new sense of solidarity for the 99 percent. International economic institutions, such as the International Monetary Fund (IMF), the World Bank, and the World Trade Organization (WTO), have served and protected the interests of the advanced industrialized countries. To be more precise, they have protected the interests of the 1 percent in those countries, as the masses in the industrialized countries are not benefiting from economic gain, while the elites in poor nations are often doing quite well. In the late 1990s, the failed neoliberal economic policies of the IMF exacerbated a financial crisis that spread from Asia to Russia and Latin America and brought the world to the precipice of a global meltdown. Financial crises in the United States and in Europe, linked to failed policies of neoliberal capitalism, wreaked havoc in the global economy.

Economic recovery has been slow, and even the citizens of the industrialized nations are feeling the pinch of austerity measures. While the economy continues to go in cycles, fewer and fewer people are benefiting even when the economic indicators rise. People who are left out of the gains of economic globalization have to struggle even harder to feed themselves and their families. The current global economic system has proven to be increasingly unstable and ecologically unsustainable, has caused social unrest, and has exacerbated ethnic and religious conflicts.

The multitude has not remained silent and passive. As global capital controls and negatively affects more and more of people's lives, the multitude has sprung into action in many protests and resistance movements to fight for their survival and for a political voice and economic change. During the Asian economic crisis in the late 1990s, protest movements spread across many Asian countries. In Latin America, the Zapatista movement in Chiapas, Mexico, galvanized indigenous peoples to fight for their rights and dignity, and also inspired new ways of forming political communities in which collective and horizontal decisions are made. More recently, labor movements have become more active again in national and international contexts. Factory workers in China, for instance, including those who work in multinational factories such as Foxconn, have staged numerous protests to demand fair compensation, job security, and safer and more humane working conditions.[6]

Globalization can be seen from above if we focus on transnational capital, multinational corporations, the international financial and monetary organizations, and the support from dominant cultural and religious forces. But there is also globalization from below, or "grassroots globalization," as anthropologist Arjun Appadurai has called it. In a widely cited essay, Appadurai outlines the characteristics of globalization from below and calls attention to the emergent social and cultural forms of the grassroots. Globalization from below consists of various social forms that have emerged to contest, interrogate, or reverse the negative effects of globalization on behalf of the world's majority who are socially and fiscally at risk.[7] It seeks to "create forms of knowledge transfer and social mobilization that proceed independently of the actions of corporate capital and the nation-state system (and its international affiliates and guarantors)."[8] The success of globalization from below requires the collaboration of many social actors, including nongovernmental organizations, transnational advocacy networks, global forums, and socially concerned academics and activists. (In this book, we are particularly interested in the contributions of religion and religious communities.) Globalization from below is constantly in flux, with disjunctive flows of capital, media images, persons, objects, and discourses. Globalization from below also requires a new imagination of social life to provide inspiration for collective dissent and to nurture new patterns of collective life. Finally, according to Appadurai, public intellectuals and progressive academics have important roles to play because they can provide information about mobile global forms of social and civic life, and they can help grassroots groups to look at their local struggles through global lenses and connect with transnational networks.

Appadurai's ideas of globalization from below offer insights into the global groundswell of protests and demonstrations of 2011, which continues to the present. When Tunisian Mohamed Bouazizi set himself on fire, probably no one would have forecast that his death would lead to mass protests in Tunisia and elsewhere in the Arab world. The multitude gathered at Egypt's Tahrir Square and the eventual ousting of President Hosni Mubarak raised global awareness that new civic and social forms are not utopian dreams—they are actually possible. "Arab spring" became a catchphrase for demands for democracy, social participation, and radical change. A new culture of social activism and mobilization swept across the globe as people watched the protests in real time on the Internet through social networks and live-streams. Protesters exchanged ideas and strategies about how to organize and resist the larger structures of oppression as well as the immediate pressures imposed upon them by the police, elite tactical teams, and the military both locally and transnationally.

The Occupy movement has succeeded in mobilizing many sectors of the multitude. In the United States, Sarah van Gelder notes that the movement "is reaching people who are carrying a protest sign for the first time, including some conservatives, along with union members who have been fighting a losing battle to maintain their standard of living."[9] Hundreds of thousands have participated in protests and occupations, and many more support the Occupy movement's key issues. Those who have participated include students and graduates (many of whom cannot find work), veterans, elderly people, the homeless, peace and social justice activists, members of the military, and people of faith. Some participants are unemployed, but many others have a day job and show up after work. The diversity of the multitude is its strength, because the movement cannot be easily pigeonholed. Different Occupy groups have their local concerns and issues, in addition to the national and global causes that they support. The members of these groups are learning to work together, to set their own pace, and to collaborate with other groups.

The Occupy movement has set up encampments in parks and public spaces. The protesters have met in other public spaces, such as libraries, churches, community halls, and civic centers. They have demonstrated on college and university campuses, staged protests in front of statehouses and government buildings, marched on bridges, and occupied foreclosed homes. In doing so, they have reappropriated spaces, around which they have created new shared ways of life and laid the groundwork for new freedom. John Allen, a protest chaplain at Occupy Wall Street, speaks of the transitory space created:

> Zuccotti Park in Lower Manhattan has become the epicenter of a struggle over space in the past few days. As protesters demand to remain encamped in the small park, seeking a space for their bodies and their voices. The city has demanded they leave. . . . A transitory space that would only stay open for so long. . . . But a space for people to move in and move through, to create a new community. To create a new future. [10]

Space is not just a matter of actual physical location. The protesters create space physically and virally, forming a World Wide Web of social networks that have not existed before. With the effective use of Facebook, Twitter, and other social networking sites, the mobile multitude has used and created innovative forms of social life and fostered an emerging global circuit of mobile civic and political expressions. During the spring of 2012, after most Occupy encampments had been shut down by the police, the actions of the so-called "99 Percent Spring" continued the trajectories of the movement. [11] Spatial presence is still important as the Occupy movement takes to the streets, particularly in marches, demonstrations, and public presentations, but the movement is not tied to a limited form of organizing.

The Occupy movement has also facilitated alternative forms of the globalization of knowledge that run counter to the dominant globalization of knowledge. Occupy Boston, for instance, set up a Free School University to provide education for the protesters and members of the community and hosted a Howard Zinn Memorial Lecture Series featuring radical thinkers such as Noam Chomsky, who has critiqued American imperialism. International progressive academic and public figures such as Judith Butler, Angela Davis, Naomi Klein, Gayatri Chakravorty Spivak, Cornel West, and Slavoj Žižek made their way to various Occupy campsites and spoke to the protesters. Their speeches have been broadcast on YouTube, posted on websites, retweeted, and collected in publications for wide circulation. Those who participated in demonstrations against the WTO and in the popular uprisings in the Middle East and Europe shared their experiences and tactics with protesters in the Occupy movement. Others who had experience in grassroots organizing in Latin America and elsewhere, particularly in the Zapatista movement, shared with their listeners the ideas of horizontal network and direct action. The Occupy movement has also trained many people in the strategies of nonviolent action and taught lessons gleaned from protests from other parts of the world.

DIRECT DEMOCRACY

Some commentators have said that the United States does not need a "Tahrir moment" because, unlike many Middle Eastern countries, the United States is a democratic country. They have criticized the Occupy movement for occupying public spaces and organizing mass rallies, and they have told the protesters to work through existing political structures. People in the Occupy movement are fully supportive of democracy, but many consider American democracy to be deeply flawed, for it works to the advantage of the 1 percent rather than the 99 percent. For this reason, the Occupy movement has not coordinated with the Republican and the Democratic parties and is skeptical of claims of representation by elected officials. Instead of trying to fix the existing system of governance, the Occupy movement has opted to experiment with something new. Marina Sitrin, one of the early organizers of Occupy Wall Street, writes, "Most of us believe that what is most important is to open space for conversations—for democracy—real, direct, and participatory democracy."[12]

Democracy has often been discussed in terms of its Greek roots and its development into representative government in the modern West. What is overlooked is the fact that Greek democracy was developed by the elites for the elites, so that many members of society were excluded. Some of this legacy is reflected in the history of the United States, where initially only white male owners of property enjoyed voting rights and even today the political influence of the common people remains limited. Nevertheless, Western liberal democracy has often been held up as the model for the rest of the world to follow and emulate, and the United States has assumed the mantle of the champion of the free world. In the name of democracy, the United States has used military force and other pressures to topple foreign governments in what has been called "regime change," though some of these governments were elected by their own people. If we examine the democratic structures of the United States, we can see that they are far from perfect. The

voting rights of minorities and the elderly are handled restrictively by pass-
ing laws requiring a government-issued ID in order to vote, redistricting is
used as a tool to maintain the political status quo, and long lines in minority
neighborhoods discourage people from voting. At the same time, the interests
of the 1 percent are served by both political parties. Tax rates for the wealthy
and corporations are at a record low, and the number of lobbyists in politics
has grown exponentially.

The Occupy movement puts the spotlight on the malfunction of the
American democratic system and the influence of global neoliberal governance structures, which favor corporations and the 1 percent. Protesters took
to the streets, parks, and public spaces to exercise the power of the people, on
which democracy rests, and to participate in direct democracy. Through concrete actions, they asserted their right to appear in public and to determine
their own affairs, and they refused to give in to harassment by the police or
the state. The multitude creates a public sphere as an alternative to the contemporary nation-state, which is dominated by the interests of the 1 percent
and upheld against the interests of the 99 percent. As Judith Butler has noted,
"One crucial and central operation of sovereign power is the capacity to
suspend the rights of individuals or groups or to cast them out of a polity."[13]
By assembling in tent-cities, marching across New York's Brooklyn Bridge,
sleeping on sidewalks, and singing in courts to disrupt proceedings for home
foreclosures, the protesters tried out and exercised their freedom.

The practice of direct democracy in the Occupy movement is not without
precedent. One significant influence are the Zapatistas of Chiapas, who rose
up in 1994 to publicly denounce the North American Free Trade Agreement
(NAFTA). The Zapatistas confronted the global neoliberal economic project,
the national structure of the Mexican state, and the dominance of the Creole-
white and even Mestizo superiority. Their movement sparked the imagination of many people around the world, and by the late 1990s many other
groups emerged that rejected hierarchical power by forming political communities in which collective and horizontal decisions were made. Such
groups included the Direct Action Network in the United States (formed after
the Seattle protest of the WTO), social forums in Italy, and neighborhood
assemblies in Argentina in the 2000s. The World Social Forums and revitalized labor movements are also part of these developments. In 2011, protesters in Greece, Spain, Tel Aviv, Hong Kong, Canada, the United States, and
many other countries rose up, demanding to be heard and to be able to
participate in the democratic process.

Looking at the Occupy movement through an international lens avoids the danger of assessing the democratic movement through Eurocentric or Euro-American lenses. In his monumental work *Politics of Liberation: A Critical World History*, Enrique Dussel points to the limits of Hellenocentric and Eurocentric interpretation of political philosophies. He writes, "When speaking of *demo*-cracy one forgets that demos signifies in Egyptian 'village'; it is neither a Greek word nor 'Indo-European.'"[14] He also cautions against privileging the theories of European political philosophers (Hobbes, Locke, Rousseau, Kant, and Marx, etc.), which often goes hand in hand with ignorance of and disdain for ideas and theories from other cultures, including the politics of Egyptian, Mesopotamian, Chinese, Hindu, and Islamic cultures, as well as the politics of Aztec, Mayan, and Incan societies.[15] Reconfiguring politics and debates about modernity in world history, Dussel's work is an inspiration for us as he seeks to expand our horizons to encompass people's movements for liberation from many historical and geographical locations.

The Occupy movement is often described as a leaderless movement, meaning that there are no easily identifiable leading figures or spokespersons. Decisions are made in the general assembly through a consensus-based decision-making process. Stephen Gandel describes the general assembly in this way:

> Facilitators run the meetings, but anyone is allowed to sign up to make proposals. Crowd members show approval by holding their hands up and wiggling their fingers. Downward wiggling fingers means you don't approve. Anyone can raise a finger to make a point. Rolling fingers means it's time to wrap up. Since no bullhorns are allowed, the crowd repeats everything every speaker says, a technique dubbed the "people's mike."[16]

He notes that at a time when people are frustrated with the government, the general assembly gives them a better sense of democracy. Such open and participatory processes allow more people to engage in the movement and feel that they are a part of it and have some ownership of it. When the number of people attending a general assembly gets too large (sometimes in the thousands), a smaller spokescouncil is formed to make some of the decisions. In addition to meeting regularly, the Occupy movement organizes a network of dozens of working groups so that participants can focus on particular tasks. These working groups carry out the day-to-day activities, focusing on concrete issues such as food, shelter, and legal assistance, as well as art, education, the role of women, facilitation, and mediation. The groups decide what they want to do and how they want to do it and do not take marching orders from any person on top. In this way, these groups empower people to take direct action in the world and to adopt diverse tactics to change the world around them.

The "leaderless" organization of the Occupy movement follows principles of radical democracy that are also found in some anarchist and democratic socialist traditions. The goal is not to replicate hierarchical forms of power, but to create a new democratic form of expression; the Occupy movement does not aim to replicate the current forms of state power, but to form decentralized and horizontal networks of self-governing institutions from below and to hold those who have state power accountable. Marina Sitrin, who has written several books on horizontalism, describes it this way:

> The concept of horizontalism embodies a critique of hierarchy and authority, but it is more than that. It is about creating new relationships. The means are a part of the ends. It is not a question of making demands, but rather the process, which is a manifestation of an alternative way of being and relating. [17]

If another world is possible, it is not enough for people to criticize the old institutions without creating something new and living in it. The Occupy movement represents a deep democratic awakening and a commitment to create a better world in which justice and compassion are practiced in new ways. The veteran activists Staughton Lynd and Andrej Grubacic have rightly said, "How can we expect people to hunger and thirst for something new and different if they have never had even a moment to experience it, to taste it, to live inside it?" [18]

By sharing power horizontally, the Occupy movement releases the potential of people to claim their agency and create something entirely new. Jennifer Wilder, a protest chaplain at Occupy Wall Street, says, "We are talking about developing leadership. Increasingly, the leaders are people who have been transformed and found an identity in the 99 percent." [19] Instead of calling it a "leaderless" movement, some have alternatively chosen to describe it as a "leaderfull" movement. The progressive activist Ilyse Hogue was one of the first to use the term "leaderfull":

We should all strive not for leaderless movements, but for leaderFULL movements. The former trends towards autocratic loudest voices dominating. In their best manifestation, the latter creates equitable space to raise up all voices, create mechanisms for group decision making and accountability, and to catalyze self-responsibility and empowerment. [20]

In other words, the Occupy movement encourages the agency and the participation of all of its members, particularly the ones who would not be traditionally considered leaders.

Cornel West, a prominent African American public intellectual, has been calling for such a democratic awakening and accountability for thirty years. A favorite among the Occupy protesters, he has spoken in New York, Boston, Los Angeles, and other places where the movement is located. The Occupy movement, for West, is a resurrection of the spirit of the Rev. Martin Luther King Jr., Rabbi Abraham Joshua Heschel, Dorothy Day, Philip Berrigan, and Cesar Chavez. West commends the protesters for their hunger for meaning, thirst for justice, and commitment to building a healthy democracy. The movement has a spiritual, a political, and also a social dimension, he notes, because "there are these wonderful bonds that are being created, communities being constituted right there at those sites."[21] These bonds, we should add, are what accounts for the religious dimension as well, as religion has to do with relationship.

The encampments became festive spaces, as protesters created a culture of democracy involving arts, drum circles, songs, poetry readings, puppets, street theater, and the savvy use of media. The emergent political culture had its own rhetoric, symbolic forms, imageries, leadership, insiders and outsiders, cultural brokers, and political networks. [22] Judith Butler has written about a notion of politics as performative, which is very significant in funding new possibilities of social and political life. [23] The protesters engage in performative politics when they sing, hold assemblies, share food with the homeless, take care of the sick and mentally ill, and set up libraries in public spaces in defiance of rulings that do not allow them to congregate. The use of the people's mike becomes a pedagogical tool in the training for democracy because performative speech is echoed in the public, and people respect and repeat the words spoken, even though they may not agree with them.

The Occupy movement's political culture is created not only on the ground but also through the Internet in livestreams, websites, blogs, wikis, YouTube, Facebook, Twitter, and other social networks. The Internet has enabled the formation of new and fluid global communities, breaking down physical and geographical barriers. The ways that people gather, relate to one another, and share information have taken many new forms. For instance, Yonatan Levi, a young organizer in Tel Aviv, imagines assemblies in chat rooms:

> I think these assemblies are chat rooms, wide open, with this sense of nonhier-archy, that everyone is equal in the kingdom of the Internet, where there are no kings or queens. We've taken these tools that we've acquired unknowingly—this generation of ours, which was blamed for not doing anything in the world—and now we've taken these things we've learned out into the street. And it's pretty impressive, I must say.[24]

Although things are not quite as ideal as Levi envisions, the Internet allows new kinds of sharing and collaboration that we could not even imagine a generation ago. For the first time in human history, we have tools that enable us to network more broadly beyond our confinement in space and, to some degree, even time. Interactive telecommunications professor Clay Shirky argues that the Internet has democratized production and distribution so much that "everyone is a media outlet."[25] Digital technology has the potential to support the self-organizing of many people from the bottom up, a model that has already radically changed consumption patterns (e.g., eBay), industries (e.g., open-source software), and knowledge production (e.g., Wikipedia) in ways that are more democratic, although the patterns of neoliberal capitalism still shine through on occasion. Digital technology has also changed the ways of political organizing because people can connect with others anywhere in the world who have access to the Internet to share ideas and strategies and to take some kind of public action together. Cultural historian Steven Johnson says, "For any movement that aims to be truly global in scope, making it almost impossible to rely on centralized power, adaptive self-organization may well be the only road available."[26] This self-organizing principle can be seen both in the campsites on the ground and in the interlinked pathways of the Internet.

One example of adaptation and change can be found in the launching of Occupy the Hood. Democracy must be understood as a long-term project in the United States, and the civil rights movement has made progress in increasing the participation of racial and ethnic minorities. Nevertheless, the level of this participation is still at risk, linked to the fact that much of minorities' economic gains have been wiped out in the past several years. Job loss and foreclosures are rampant in communities of color. Since the Occupy movement initially was overwhelmingly populated by young white people, even in some of the country's most diverse cities (such as New York), black activists organized Occupy the Hood in September 2011 to bring more people of color and their concerns to the Occupy movement. Like Occupy Wall Street, Occupy the Hood got its online start with a call to action, and the group spread its words through Facebook and Twitter.[27] Occupy Wall Street also joined forces with Occupy the Dream, an effort to link the Poor People's Campaign of the Rev. Martin Luther King Jr., disrupted by his assassination, to the present crisis affecting disproportionately people of color.

Even after the police raided various encampments, working groups continued to meet but fewer people attended the general assemblies. It is too soon to know what forms and directions this experiment in direct democracy will take. Looking to the future, Hardt and Negri ask, "How can we transform indignation and rebellion into a lasting constituent process? How can experiments in democracy become a constituent power, not only democratizing a public square or a neighborhood but also inventing an alternative society that is really democratic?"[28] No one has all the answers, but by asking these questions, new solutions can be found through creative and collaborative innovation. Religion, as we hope to show in this book, has its own particular contributions to make.

CRITICS AND CULTURAL BROKERS

Not surprisingly, the Occupy movement has attracted its fair share of criticism from right-leaning politicians and conservative commentators. During the presidential primary season, Mitt Romney repeatedly stated that the language of the 1 percent and the 99 percent was inciting "class warfare." The right course, according to Romney, is not to pit Americans against each other, but to bring the American people together. The unanswered question is, of course, who pits Americans against each other at this time in history. The most caustic remarks came from former House speaker Newt Gingrich. At a Republican presidential forum in Iowa in November 2011, he told the occupiers to "go get a job, right after you take a bath,"[29] underhandedly implying that unemployment is the personal fault of the unemployed.

While politicians calibrated their remarks for political gain, reporters, commentators, talk-show hosts, bloggers, and pundits filled the airwaves with a wide range of opinions and analyses. Rush Limbaugh, the well-known

ultra-conservative radio talk-show host, was acidic and sarcastic in his comments. After the Occupy Wall Street camp was raided, Limbaugh was cele-
bratory in his tone and said, "Okay, so the good news is that the cops have
finally liberated Zuccotti Park from the occupy army, occupation of those
lousy hippies, thieves, rapists, purse snatchers, muggers who were camped
out there."[30] He added that the protesters would likely be glad to move back
in with their parents without losing face. They could go back home as heroes.

David Brooks, a *New York Times* op-ed columnist and TV news commen-
tator, thought the Occupy movement was overhyped and had received too
much media attention. He visited the movement in Minneapolis in mid-
October 2011 and found that it had only about thirty people, while the one in
Washington, DC, had about eighty. "The movement is small," Brooks wrote.
"Sure, they are photogenic, and they do have some grievances, but it is
extremely dangerous to extrapolate from the protests to the wider country."
The idea of income redistribution is not popular among the American people,
he surmised. Even in economic hard times, Americans want to see effort
linked to reward and redistribution. He also advised that in reporting about
protest movements, "Don't watch the people doing the marching. Watch the
people watching the marching."[31] Yet the line between those marching and
those watching may not be as easy to draw as Brooks would hope, as the
majority of Americans are in favor of the Occupy movement.

In an interview on CNN, Niall Ferguson, a British historian who teaches
at Harvard University, felt that we should avoid "criminalizing one percent
of the population." Ferguson has conservative political views, and his writings lend support to the grand colonizing projects undertaken by the British.
He has argued that the British Empire did much good for the world and that
he would like to see the United States embrace its imperial character because
many parts of the world would benefit from a period of American rule.[32] For
him, the Occupy movement misses the point because "the principal cause
driving inequality is globalization and not malpractice of Wall Street." What
Ferguson overlooks, of course, is that the Occupy movement makes a similar
point: the problem is not the malpractice or criminal activity of individuals
but the economic system. To bolster his argument, he has pointed out that the
American banks have problems, but so have the European banks. Some of
them were guilty of incompetence and malpractice, and others were insol-
vent. The real problem is not Wall Street, he insists, but the decline of social
mobility, an issue that has often been overlooked.[33] The unasked question is
what hampers social mobility.

Others have expressed concern whether the term "occupy" is appropriate. Angela Davis, an iconic political activist and scholar who rose to prominence in the civil rights movement, spoke at a gathering at Washington Square Park in Manhattan. She noted that occupation is usually violent and brutal and that the United States was founded on genocidal occupation of indigenous lands. Many places (for instance, Palestine) remain occupied territory, and for good reasons, the slogan of the Occupy movement in Puerto Rico is "(Un)Occupy." Nevertheless, Davis still affirmed the Occupy movement, saying, "We turn 'occupation' into something that is beautiful, something that brings community together. Something that calls for love and happiness and hope."[34]

Some Native American activists, however, find the term "occupy" too insensitive and problematic, for it overlooks the fact that the United States has occupied native lands for centuries and continues to do so. According to this persepctive, while Occupy Wall Street protesters and organizers have encouraged people to "occupy" different places that symbolize power and greed, they seem to forget that New York City is Haudenosaunee territory and home to many other First Nations. Instead of the term "occupy," they prefer to use "decolonize" instead, and they put out posters that read "Decolonize Wall Street" and "Decolonize the 99 percent." Jessica Yee (Mohawk), the executive director for the Native Youth Sexual Health Network, supports the mission and integrity of Occupy Wall Street, yet she expresses reservations. "I'm not against ending capitalism and I'm not against people organizing to hold big corporations accountable for the extreme damage they are causing," Yee writes. "Yes, we need to end globalization. What I am saying is that I have all kinds of problems when to get to 'ending capitalism' we step on other people's rights—and in this case erode Indigenous rights—to make the point."[35]

Critics are joined by cultural brokers, who help facilitate contacts with the outside world and serve as mediators between global and local interests.[36] A group of prominent intellectuals made trips to Zuccotti Park when Occupy Wall Street was in its nascent stage. Among them was Slavoj Žižek, a well-known Slovenian cultural critic and philosopher of the left. In his remarks, he placed the Occupy movement within the broader, long-term struggle of oppressed people around the world. He noted that the problem is not corruption or greed but the system, and declared, "The marriage between democracy and capitalism is over. The change is possible."[37] He challenged the occupiers to think of an alternative, worldwide system that protects the commons—

the commons of nature, the commons of knowledge, and the commons of biogenetics—and he reminded his attentive audience that "when you criticize capitalism, don't allow yourself to be blackmailed that you are against democracy."[38]

The Occupy movement has received support from many clergy and religious leaders across the United States, who have reached out to members of their faith communities. More than 1,400 church leaders, including the Rev. Jesse Jackson, had signed a pledge of support for the movement by December 2011. A coalition of prominent African American pastors signed on to join with the movement to launch a new series of actions, which they considered part of the legacy of the Rev. Martin Luther King Jr. As will be discussed in the next section, priests, rabbis, and lay religious leaders led Sabbath and worship services, meditations, and discussion groups inside the encampments and in the spirituality tents in a spirit of critical support of the movement.

When conflicts and clashes occurred between the protesters and the authorities, and between the protesters and other sectors of society, religious leaders played conspicuous roles as alternative power brokers. On October 15, 2011, thousand of protesters in London descended on an area around the London Stock Exchange in order to set up a camp similar to Occupy Wall Street outside St. Paul's Cathedral. Several days later, the cathedral's decision to close its doors because of the protest aroused strong reactions from the public. The Rev. Giles Fraser, canon chancellor of the cathedral, resigned because he could not reconcile his conscience with the possibility that the church and the City of London would evict the protesters by force. His comment, "The church cannot answer peaceful protest with violence,"[39] remains a challenge for Christianity. The doors of the cathedral were subsequently reopened, and the church decided not to pursue legal action to evict the protesters. The bishop of London, Richard Chartres, also showed sympathy for the protesters. As the City of London continued to press legal action for eviction, Archbishop Rowan Williams, leader of the Anglican Communion, wrote to the *Financial Times*, affirming that the protest was "an expression of a widespread and deep exasperation with the financial establishment."[40] Such high-profile support, although not always quite going to the bottom of the concerns of the Occupy movement, was certainly a boost to Occupy London.

In New York, after the camp at Zuccotti Park was raided, protesters in New York looked for other public spaces in which to gather. They appealed to Trinity Church, an Episcopal church on Wall Street, to allow them to set up a winter encampment on a vacant lot that the church owns at Duarte Square. Earlier, Trinity Church had provided the protesters with meeting spaces and allowed them to use the church's facilities. Bishop George E. Packard, former chaplain for the armed services and a decorated Vietnam veteran, acted as the liaison in negotiations between the church and the protesters. He had hoped that Duarte Square could be the new home for the protesters. But when the Rev. James Cooper, rector of Trinity Church, and leaders of the church decided that to allow a winter encampment on a site with no facilities would be "unsafe, unhealthy and potentially injurious," emotions rose very high. Some criticized the wealthy church for its failure to stand in solidarity with the protesters. During a tense moment, Archbishop Desmund Tutu, Nobel laureate and leader of the anti-apartheid movement in South Africa, issued a statement aimed at reconciliation. He called the Occupy movement "a voice of the world" and appealed to the church to break the impasse and help the protesters.[41] But he also said that Trinity Church had been a staunch supporter of him and Nelson Mandela during the anti-apartheid movement. His comments created some understanding of the mission and position of Trinity Church, although this did not resolve all the questions. What is the role of the church in the current life-and-death struggle with global capitalism if we take seriously the courageous position of the church in the life-and-death struggle with South African apartheid? The church is always taking sides, and the decision of Trinity Church led to the arrests of protesters who tried to occupy Duarte Square. Bishop Packard and other clergy members were among those arrested.

In addition to religious leaders, pop singers and cultural icons served as intermediaries and conduits to popular culture. Joan Baez, a folk singer-songwriter well known for singing songs like "Blowing in the Wind" during the Vietnam era, was invited to perform at Occupy Wall Street. At seventy years old, the legendary Baez encouraged the sort of mutuality that is at the heart of true democracy: "It is very important that I learn from you. You do a lot of things differently from the way we did back then, and a lot of the things the same." The presence of Baez reminded the Occupy movement of its connection to the longer history of protest movements in the United States and the dreams and visions of young people of past generations. She led the crowd in singing "Where's My Apple Pie," a song she wrote for and about the veterans of the Vietnam War in the 1970s. When she changed the final chorus to "It's time to Occupy," the people joined her with great gusto and energy.[42]

If Joan Baez represents the past, Miley Cyrus belongs to the future. The nineteen-year-old actress and singer-songwriter became a household name for starring in the Disney Channel sitcom *Hannah Montana*. During one weekend in November 2011, Occupy Wall Street got a boost of publicity because Cyrus posted a YouTube clip pairing images and videos of protests around the world with a remix of her 2010 song "Liberty Walk." The footage primarily shows the police dragging protesters on the ground, donning riot gear, and flashing their batons. The lyrics are not particularly relevant to the Occupy movement, but, as one commentator says, "One of the biggest, most recognizable pop stars in the world calling attention to and siding with a grassroots political protest is important."[43] In London, singer and songwriter Thom Yorke of Radiohead and Robert "3D" del Naja from Massive Attack, a British trip hop duo, appeared at the Christmas party of Occupy London and put on a "thank you" gig in solidarity with the movement. It went viral on the Internet.

FAITHFUL ACTION

The Occupy movement has drawn people of faith from diverse traditions to support the movement and to work together. Many progressive Buddhist, Muslim, Jewish, Protestant, Catholic, and pagan individuals and groups, as well as interfaith groups, have lent their support, resources, and facilities to the movement for the 99 percent.[44] The movement has energized the Religious Left in particular because in the past three decades in the United States, faith-based politics has been dominated by the Religious Right, and has coalesced around a very limited set of social issues, such as abortion and homosexuality. Combining religious fervor and progressive politics is not new, as Harvard political scientist Robert Putnam has observed: "It's hard to name a progressive movement in American history that did not have powerful religious allies and influences."[45] Religious symbols and ceremonies are brought to life once again in the context of progressive politics and protests in the participatory Occupy movement, continuing a tradition that goes back to Jesus and the prophets. In the United States, progressive politics and protests date back to America's Revolutionary War through the anti-slavery and civil rights movements, the labor movement, and the women's movement, and these sentiments were also manifested in protests against the Vietnam War and the more recent wars in Iraq and Afghanistan.

The Occupy movement helped ground and strengthen interfaith partnerships as Jewish rabbis; Christian priests, pastors, and chaplains; Muslim imams; and other religious leaders worked to organize prayer services, initiate meditations, and perform rituals on various campsites. "What unifies these diverse groups is a shared spiritual conviction that protesting injustice and inequality, defending the weak, and caring for the poor are key religious tenets," writes Catherine Woodiwiss.[46] In Occupy Boston, religious leaders established a "faith and spirituality tent" with religious symbols from different traditions that was open to people of all beliefs as well as nonbelievers such as humanists, agnostics, and atheists. This tent hosted Muslim prayer services, Zen Buddhist meditations, and Jewish celebrations for Yom Kippur, and provided food and shelter for those who needed them. In Occupy Wall Street, an altar was established under a big tree at one corner of Zuccotti Park. People placed images of Hindu goddesses and the Christian Virgin of Guadalupe, Buddhist images, candles, bells, rosaries, stones, and posters on the altar, creating an inclusive and respectful atmosphere for all traditions. Members from the Judson Memorial Church in New York City carried a golden calf in the shape of the Wall Street bull and marched down to Wall Street in a sarcastic protest of the "idol" of corporate greed. In Oakland, the Interfaith Tent "has been a sacred space of solace at the encampment, but it has also provided a spiritual canopy for an interfaith coalition of Indigenous Elders, Buddhists, Christians, Muslims and Jews in solidarity with the Occupy Movement, locally and globally."[47]

The movement received a boost when the Vatican released a statement on global financial reform on October 24, 2011. Although the statement does not directly talk about the Occupy movement, it finds fault with neoliberal capitalism and blames easy money and credit for the financial crisis. It also notes that globalization has brought huge benefits to many, but has left out the poor. It says that speculation has hurt the global markets and the developing world. The statement calls for the gradual creation of a world political authority to regulate the financial market and to rein in the "inequalities and distortions of capitalist development."[48] Cardinal Peter Turkson, president of the Pontifical Council for Justice and Peace, which issued the statement, said that the basic sentiment behind the Occupy movement is in line with Catholic social teaching. Both the Occupy movement and Catholic social teaching emphasize that the economy should be at the service of the human person and that strong measures must be taken to reduce the growing gap between the rich and the poor. The secretary of the council, Bishop Mario Toso, also told reporters that the new document "appears to be in line with the slogans" of Occupy Wall Street and other protest movements around the globe, but "even more it is in line with the previous teaching of the church," including Pope Benedict XVI's 2009 encyclical *Caritas in Veritate* [*Charity in Truth*].[49]

As the Occupy movement spread across cities in the United States, there was a parallel movement called Occupy Judaism. The Occupy protests provided stimulation for some Jewish people to rethink their religious institutions and to experiment with new forms of Judaism in society. Occupy Judaism is a clear signal that many Jews consider themselves to be part of the 99 percent and that they support the protests against disenfranchisement in American society. One of the organizers of Occupy Judaism, Daniel Sieradski, helped to put together an open-air Kol Nidre (all vows) service in New York to express solidarity with the Occupy movement. On October 7, 2011, hundreds of people gathered in New York and other locations for a Kol Nidre service that marked the beginning of Yom Kippur (Day of Atonement). Regina Weiss of the Jewish Funds for Justice says, "For many there is no more important way to stand up and express Judaism on the holiest night of the year than to stand with people who are hurting and to stand up for greater equality in the country."[50] The service drew many Jewish people who would otherwise not attend traditional services in the synagogues. Similar services were held in Boston, Philadelphia, and Washington, DC. During the week-long Jewish holiday Sukkot, Jewish activists erected traditional *sukkah* tents in Zuccotti Park and in campsites in several other cities amid the tarps, tents, blankets, and signs. The *sukkah* is a tent built each year during the Sukkot celebration of harvest for thanksgiving and for remembering those affected by injustice. As one Jewish protester reminded the people, Sukkot is a time to "celebrate the abundance that we have and recognize the fragility of that abundance."[51] The meaning of Sukkot was made even more relevant when the police threatened to raid the encampments.

Daniel Sieradski said, "Most of the Jewish institutions are dominated by their wealthiest donors, whose views may not be in line with that of the wider Jewish community. It is our community and our tradition as much as it is anybody's, and they need to make space for us."[52] This resonates with what many Christians have said about church institutions. Sieradski added that the

Occupy Judaism movement aims to make the Jewish tradition a "living, breathing, justice movement."[53] The traditional Jewish rituals of Kol Nidre service and Sukkot, performed in the context of the Occupy protests, expressed Jewish beliefs, heritage, and values. Rabbi Arthur Waskow, director of New York's Shalom Center, reiterates that protest is a key part of Judaism. He says, "From the Exodus, from Isaiah, from Jeremiah and all the way down to rabbinic Judaism, there is a sense that Judaism is constantly struggling against top-down power of the Pharaoh . . . Judaism calls for freedom, democracy, and feeding the hungry."[54]

Some Jewish activists in New York were concerned about and protested against a minority strain of anti-Zionism and anti-Semitism within the Occupy movement. A person was seen holding a sign stating, "Zionists control the financial world." Some people pointed out links between Israel and American imperialism, including economic imperialism, which made some members of the Jewish community uncomfortable. But there were other Jews who were very vocal against Israel's occupation of Palestine. For example, a group of young Jews called for action to "un-occupy Palestine." Their statement read, "We call for young Jews and allies nationwide to join in solidarity with Occupy Wall Street and with our Palestinian siblings living under their own form of occupation. Let us stand up to the 1 percent in our own community—the powerful institutions that support Israel's corporate-backed military control of the Palestinian people and act as the gatekeepers for our community."[55] The Occupy movement motivates these young Jews to reflect on the power dynamics within their own communities and to express their concerns for Palestinians under occupation.

Muslim leaders joined Jewish and Christian groups in support of the Occupy movement. They held prayer services in solidarity with the movement for the 99 percent. Members of the New York chapter of the Council on American Islamic Relations and the local Islamic Leadership Council came to Occupy Wall Street to express their grievances and to speak of social justice. Imam Aiyub Abdul Baki of the Islamic Leadership Council delivered a sermon on social justice based on the last sermon of the Prophet Muhammad. He referred to the Prophet's commandment against usury, a veiled reference to Wall Street bankers. He also mentioned that the suffering of Muslims based on racism and discrimination and Islam-bashing is on the rise.[56]

Other religious leaders also applied insights from the Occupy movement to look at their own traditions. Buddhist teacher and writer Lewis Richmond, for example, writes about "Occupy Buddha." He says that the word "buddha" means to wake up, and the Occupy movement and its many offshoots are a kind of global awakening. As a prince, Gautama, who later became the Buddha, belonged to the 1 percent of his time. But when he walked out of his palace, he was awakened to the suffering of poverty, sickness, death, and aging. The Jewish, Christian, and Muslim traditions share a similar memory of Moses, who was raised among the 1 percent in Egypt but was awakened when he saw a slavemaster beating one of the Hebrew slaves. Richmond is aware that some fellow Buddhists want to convey the Buddhist instructions of nonviolence, compassion, and meditation to the Occupy protesters. But he thinks people should be allowed to express anger and indignation in the fight for justice. The protesters must be appreciated, he says,

> for the truths they are speaking and the role they are playing at this critical time in the development of human consciousness. They have already discovered what the Buddha taught in his second Noble Truth—that the root cause of our unnecessary suffering is grasping, clinging, selfishness, and greed—often for money, sometimes for emotional or physical safety, nearly always for power. The energy of greed is the prime distorter of human community. The Buddha clearly saw this.[57]

Religious leaders of denominations have preached, written, and issued statements in support of the protest. For instance, the president of the Unitarian Universalist Association, the Rev. Peter Morales, said in a statement, "Unitarian Universalism embodies a long tradition of working for economic justice and workers' rights. Today is another opportunity for us to live out our faith, and the Occupy protests are a first step on the road to repairing our country."[58] Mardi Tindal, moderator of the United Church of Canada, wrote a blog titled *Occupy Hope*, in which she said, "I'm deeply moved by all that I've seen of United Church members and leaders who are actively participating in on-the-ground community efforts to seek justice and participate in God's healing and mending work toward abundant life for all. The occupy movement is yet another expression of our hope."[59] Local congregations and churches provided food and water and offered spaces for the protesters to meet and use their facilities.

Religious leaders and activists have also organized Occupy Faith groups in different cities, which provide an opportunity for people to discuss the role of faith in the Occupy movement. An Occupy Faith National Gathering was convened at Judson Memorial Church in New York City in December 2011, and it issued a statement. The statement began by saying, "As people from various faith and spiritual communities, we find in the OWS [Occupy Wall Street] Movement a Waking Force that has dispelled despair, depression, and denial about the gross injustices of society and the suffering of our people."[60] The religious leaders and activists stood in solidarity with engaged and transforming actions designed to bring about open democracy, fair justice systems, just economic policies, quality education for all, affordable housing, strong environmental policies, peace among nations, hospitality for immigrants, and transformative and creative works of human imagination and freedom.

In March 2012, another Occupy Faith National Gathering was held in East Bay and Oakland, California, with sixty conference participants from fourteen Occupy locations in the United States. The gathering was facilitated by Asian American theologian and activist Rita Nakashima Brock. The majority of the participants were Christians but there were also Buddhists, Jews, Muslims, Native Americans, Wiccans, atheists, and agnostics, as well as people who identified with multiple religious traditions. During the gathering people exchanged stories of supporting local Occupy sites and planned coordinated national Occupy Faith activities for the future.[61] Brock urged religious leaders to organize study groups and discuss with their congregations the values and issues behind the Occupy movement and the core and moral issues around injustice.

Protest chaplains in Boston, New York, Washington, DC, and other cities planned interfaith rituals, led study groups, provided pastoral counseling, and helped to resolve conflicts in the campsites. Protest chaplain John Allen also noted that the chaplains in Occupy Wall Street had good relations with the medical working group, which would refer to the chaplains people who had mental issues or needed somebody to talk to. The nonviolence coordinating group provided people with nonviolence training and ensured that people understood the rules for staying in the camps. But after sleeping for some twenty days on the ground in these camps, people were on edge. The chaplains would intervene in conflicts and tried to separate people who engaged in fights. They also spoke with people late in the night who felt lonely and wanted company.[62] The protest chaplains wore badges with their names and the words "protest chaplains," and those we talked to had different under-standings of their roles and identities. Some thought that they were there to perform particular pastoral roles without being part of the movement. Others felt that they were part of the 99 percent; they participated as fully as others in the Occupy movement, and even risked being arrested. They saw that they were called to provide pastoral care and accompaniment, but this did not separate them from others.

The Rev. Stephanie Shockley, an Episcopal priest and a hospital chaplain in New York, went from being a chaplain to the Occupy movement to being an occupier whose role was to be a chaplain. Like many others, she wit-nessed many acts of police brutality and continued to provide pastoral care and support for men and women who were arrested. She observed that some-times these people were beaten or hurt during the arrest and that many of them were severely traumatized. Members of the Occupy movement used Facebook and Twitter to share information of when the protesters would be released from custody. They would arrange for someone to meet them and bring them food, clothing, and supplies, and ensure that they had medical care, access to lawyers, and a place to stay for the night, if necessary. Shock-ley noted that these experiences helped her to understand better the Gospel imperative to visit those imprisoned. In ancient times, there was no provision for food and clothing in jails, and prisoners would experience hardship if no one visited and brought these necessities to them.[63]

The Occupy movement prompted a new level of discussion among stu-dents of theology and religion in many colleges, universities, divinity schools, and seminaries. In Boston, for example, students in the various divinity schools gathered with faculty and administrators to reflect together on religion and social movements, the church and social action, and strate-gies for democratic involvement and nonviolent action. A website, *Theology Salon*, was set up to exchange ideas and views about whether the Occupy movement might need the support of theologians and whether theology itself might need occupying. The different postings include labor and work in Catholic social teaching, human dignity and the Occupy movement, occupa-tion, compassion, and justice. Some graduate students organized the event "Occupy@AAR/SBL," which took place at the annual meeting of the American Academy of Religion (AAR) and Society of Biblical Literature (SBL) in November 2011. The conversation began not with theoretical re-flections but with reports from people involved in the various Occupy move-ments throughout the United States and Canada. In a second part, five short statements were presented, addressing the need to deal with the Occupy movement not as scholars of religion and theology observing it from the outside but rather from the inside, located within the dichotomy of the 1 percent and the 99 percent. These examples demonstrate that the Occupy movement challenges not only politics and economics but also the churches and academic institutions, where top-down power is often just as prominently at work.

Finally, the involvement and witnessing of people of faith in the Occupy movement challenge us to rethink our most deeply held commitments and beliefs and to speak about God and faith anew in our present time. The multitude that has now sprung into action provides inspiration for a public theology that embraces diversity, seeks justice, and challenges models of religious community that distance churches, mosques, and synagogues from civil engagement. The multitude further challenges models of divinity that cast God in the image of the 1 percent. As Rita Nakashima Brock has said, "Occupying is the spiritual heart of the movement. It is how people with a fierce desire for a different world embody, in real life practices, the community life they want. In all its imperfections and struggles, the Occupy Movement embodies respect for the earth, generosity and care for others, open democracy, appreciation for diversity and an ethos of love."[64] To be sure, this ethos of love includes the tough love of taking a stand on the side of the 99 percent of humanity, the exploited earth, and the divine that has resisted cooptation. This love is what requires us to address the conflicts that mark our age, as the rule of the 1 percent increasingly affects all of life.

Chapter Four

Theology of the Multitude

And [Jesus] came forth and saw a great multitude, and he had compassion on
them, because they were as sheep not having a shepherd: and he began to teach
them many things.

> —Mark 6:34 (American Standard Version)

LIFE-AND-DEATH MATTERS

The world as a whole is facing an unprecedented crisis. While living standards have increased for some, inequality is more pronounced today than
ever before and affects more people than ever. Large and growing parts of
humanity are forced to struggle for survival every day, even in the wealthiest
countries. Inequality in the United States, a country that often takes pride in
being the leader for others to emulate, is especially troublesome. In Dallas,
Texas, for instance, nearly one in four residents are already living in poverty,
and the number is rising.[1] This amounts to a struggle of life and death.

Moreover, the world is facing an unprecedented crisis because our environment is pulled into this life-and-death struggle. Global warming may not
erase life on earth altogether, but many life forms are faced with extinction as
the polar ice caps are melting, sea levels are rising, and climate is changing
due to actions by humans. While this may not mean the end of humanity as a
species, the people hit hardest will be those who do not have the means to
protect themselves from severe weather and pollution. In addition to these
large-scale changes, harmful destruction of the environment as a result of
uncontrolled exploitation of resources continues at unprecedented levels.

Forests continue to be destroyed in ecologically sensitive areas like the rain-forests, and mineral resources are extracted through techniques like fracking and hilltop removal, which were unimaginable just a few years ago.

These problems are not merely social in nature. They are theological at their very core because they are tied up with the ruling classes putting them-selves in what is often considered to be God's place. These are the people who maintain dominant power and who benefit the most from the way things are. An old definition of sin illustrates this problem. When Augustine talked about the sin of pride in the fifth century, he had in mind human beings playing God. The Roman Empire of his time and the growth of an imperial church provided plenty of examples. Today, we know that pride is not neces-sarily the problem of humanity as a whole, but the problem of the 1 percent who have the power and the means to create the world in their image and for their interests. Many working people, women, and minorities are never given the opportunity to play God, as we are reminded of our bondage every day. Members of the middle class perceive ourselves as closer to the 1 percent and share in a certain level of pride, but the truth is that the system is chipping away at our positions at an alarming rate, and we need to wake up before it is too late.[2]

The theological nature of these life-and-death struggles has often been forgotten even in the theological traditions that continue to take seriously the utterly destructive nature of sin. The theological lesson we must learn is that those who put themselves in the place of God are putting themselves in the place of an idol. The all-controlling God who acts from the top down, alone and without inviting the participation of the people and without the need to listen to anyone, is not the God of Jesus Christ or the people of Israel. We have to sound the warning of Anselm of Canterbury in the eleventh century, who, in conversation with his student Boso, famously said, "You have not yet considered the weight of sin."

In the midst of this deepening crisis that is becoming increasingly a mat-ter of life and death, theology is not a luxury, but finds itself at the heart of efforts to present alternative ways and solutions. If another world is possible, as the World Social Forums have stated, another theology may be possible as well. And another theology, in turn, will contribute to another world. While the powers that be keep telling us that there is no alternative—this has been the message of empires throughout history and is internalized to a greater degree today than ever before—we maintain that alternatives exist and that theology can help us to identify them.

The good news is that we do not have to start from scratch. Alternative theologies have been around since the days of old, and many fresh approaches have been developed in recent decades. We explicitly acknowledge our gratitude to the various liberation theologies in all parts of the world—Latin America, Africa, Asia, Europe, Oceania, North America—and to theologies in the feminist, womanist (African American women), and *mujerista* (Hispanic/Latina) traditions. We are also indebted to queer, postcolonial, and subaltern theologies, and the theologies of minorities, including Latinos/Latinas, African Americans, Asian Americans, Native Americans and First Nations, and others in North America. This list could be continued. In addition, religious traditions throughout history have contributed not only to resistance against empire and oppressive powers but also to new, constructive approaches. In the eighteenth century, for instance, early Methodism was shaped in close connection with the labor movement in England and abolitionist sentiment in the United States.[3] Evangelical traditions, in a curious reversal of mainstream evangelicalism today, promoted alternative ways of life and egalitarian relationships, including the ordination of women.[4] In Roman Catholicism, monastic movements like the Franciscans, founded in the early Middle Ages, have upheld some of the ideals of the founders, like the value of poverty, and in more recent decades the Catholic Worker movement has made a notable difference.

While we are grateful for all these traditions, which have provided important challenges and insights, we have to push further today for the sake of survival of a large part of humanity and the planet. We have to bring together many of these alternative concerns in order to push together for a new world in ways that respect the substantial diversity of all these approaches. Today it is clearer than ever that a single group cannot accomplish the needed transformations, and we need each other more now than at any other time in history. Facing the pressures surrounding us, we see no other way forward than to unite, while maintaining respect for the differences among us. For these reasons, we are proposing a theology of the multitude.

THE MULTITUDE IN THEOLOGICAL TERMS

"Multitude" is a term that symbolizes this coming together in ways that respect different traditions, cultures, and ways of life. "The multitude" stands for what has often been described as unity in difference. "Multitude" is a

term that describes a deep concern of the biblical traditions. At the heart of
the Jesus movement was not what has often been referred to as the *demos* of
the Greeks, the assembly of privileged citizens from which the word "democracy" comes. At the heart of this movement were the *laos* and the *ochlos*,
both of which describe the common people in contrast with the privileged
citizens of the empire or of the religious elites. *Laos* is a term used for a
broader group of people than the privileged *demos*. In the New Testament,
the term *laos* refers to the common people. It speaks of "the new *laos* of God
[that] incarnates not a nation but a multitude, a 'popular' people, a new
experience of humanity without exclusions."[5] *Ochlos* in the New Testament
means a "crowd, multitude, the common people."[6] Korean *minjung* theology
focuses especially on *ochlos* in the Gospels and in the Pauline writings.
According to Korean New Testament scholar Ahn Byung Mu (1922–1996),
the *ochlos* in Mark's Gospel gathered and followed Jesus and formed the
background of Jesus's activities (Mark 2:4, 2:13, 3:9, 3:20, 3:32, 4:1, 5:21,
5:24, 5:31, 8:1, 10:1). The *ochlos* were against the rulers, and they were
clearly on Jesus's side, in contrast to the ruling class from Jerusalem, which
attacked and criticized Jesus (Mark 2:4–7, 3:2–22, 11:18, 11:27, 11:32). The
Galilean *ochlos*, as amorphous and diverse groups of people from the lower
class, represents those whom Jesus's message addresses. The call to follow
him is not only for the twelve disciples but also for the *ochlos* as a whole
(Mark 8:34).[7] Members of the *laos* and *ochlos* assembled for the most part
outside the established institutions, in fields, on mountains, and by the water.

By adopting the term "multitude," we want to acknowledge the contributions of Korean *minjung* theology, which has often been overlooked in the
West. The term *minjung* can be translated as "multitude," and it combines
several of our concerns. Of particular importance in the United States, *minjung* reminds us of the notion of class, a concept often avoided in our context,
but that is now promoted by the Occupy movement. *Minjung* theologians
have pointed out the parallel between *minjung* and the *ochlos* in the New
Testament. Jesus identified his work with the *ochlos*, and they were the ones
who went to hear him speak and to witness his healing. Jesus accepted and
supported them, and he was criticized for associating with them since they
were the marginalized and alienated class.[8]

Unlike traditional preachers who present good ideas from elevated positions like pulpits and lecterns, Jesus not only preached to the multitude but
organized it as well. As Richard A. Horsley has pointed out, this was one of
the key reasons why the representatives of the Roman Empire, both political

and religious ones, wanted to get rid of Jesus, the son of Joseph. His contemporary, the peasant prophet Jesus, the son of Hananiah, who went around delivering oracles of judgment and deliverance, was merely beaten by the Romans and set free because they believed that he was deranged.[9]

In addition to the significance of the term "multitude" in our theological traditions, the idea of the multitude has also been prominent in current debates about resistance to empire and domination. Michael Hardt and Antonio Negri, in particular, have provided some insightful definitions and distinctions that help us deepen our theological reflections. In contrast to the term "the people," which often tends to describe a unified group, "the multitude" allows for and welcomes differences among various members. In contrast to the term "the masses," which tends to level the difference of those who are part of it, "the multitude" invites differences of expression, multiple identities, and shades of colors and hues of its parts.

The multitude picks up the concerns of working people, the so-called working class, because it values the notion of production. While the multitude is forced to endure the pressures of the system, it does not remain passive. Working people make substantial contributions to society, which are often overlooked and underappreciated. Hardt and Negri extend the multitude to the unemployed, unpaid domestic laborers, and the poor, who also make substantial contributions to society. We agree with their idea that "the multitude gives the concept of the proletariat its fullest definition as all those who labor and produce under the rule of capital."[10] This understanding of the multitude matches many biblical and liberation theology traditions, according to which the *laos* and the *ochlos* are not primarily the recipients of welfare but rather agents who make a difference. Marginalized women, for instance, make a difference in ways that the status quo would never expect. In one of Jesus's parables, a widow's stubborn insistence and refusal to accept any other outcome persuades an unjust judge to grant her justice (Luke 18:1–8). In the story of another widow offering all that she has to the poor, though she herself has little to give, Jesus compares her dedication to the shallowness of the wealthy (Mark 12:41–44). And a Gentile Syrophoenician woman does what systematic theologians of the status quo have always thought to be impossible: she changes Jesus's mind (Mark 7:24–30).

While the multitude is productive in surprising and unexpected ways, those who live parasitic lives have excluded themselves from the multitude. Against common opinion, parasitic lives are lived not by the poor and the unemployed but by the rulers, who siphon off the wealth of the multitude for their own individual enjoyment.[11] Jesus cautioned his followers, "You know that among the Gentiles those whom they recognize as their rulers lord it over them, and their great ones are tyrants over them. But it is not so among you; but whoever wishes to be great among you must be your servant, and whoever wishes to be the first among you must be slave of all" (Mark 10:42–44).

For good reasons, Hardt and Negri focus on economic class, in part because this concept has not received enough attention in recent debates, but also because the multitude needs to be understood in terms of economic production. It is both the "common subject of labor, that is, the real flesh of postmodern production," and "the object from which collective capital tries to make the body of its global development."[12] As the multitude is constituted by labor, it is unified by outside pressures: "Capital wants to make the multitude into an organic unity, just like the state wants to make it into a people." This forced unification, however, can be used by the multitude to its advantage, for "through the struggles of labor, the real productive biopolitical figure of the multitude begins to emerge." Since capital is not limited to what happens at work—"it extends throughout society well beyond the factory walls and geographically throughout the globe"[13]—we need to keep in mind the broader ramifications of economic matters, which ultimately include religion.

We argue that religious and theological reflections have a role to play not because the religious world is untainted by and independent of the world of capital, but because alternatives present themselves in the midst of the pressures of life. Confronted with the life-and-death struggles of our age, we are experiencing what has been called "grace under pressure."[14] A theological surplus emerges where we least expect it, not in spiritual retreats to the mountaintops or in individual enlightenment in isolation, but in the midst of struggle.

In order for theology to contribute to alternatives, it must confront the ways that religious sentiments and concepts have been used to reinforce the top-down domination of the 1 percent. Capitalism's faith in the so-called invisible hand of the market, which benefits the large corporations and the wealthy far more than the 99 percent, is only the tip of the iceberg.[15] The notion of sin, even if not always used explicitly, is usually turned against the multitude. People who are unemployed are portrayed as idle and lazy, and the contributions of working people are devalued and downplayed so that their wages and benefits can be slashed and their jobs sent overseas. Participants in the Occupy movement have been treated similarly, as they are also accused of being lazy and parasitic, and they are frequently criminalized by the media and the authorities.

THE MULTITUDE-IN-RELATION

The multitude is all about relationship. This may sound like an odd claim in a world that has been shaped by the individualism of neoliberal capitalism. Over three decades, neoliberal capitalism has successfully promoted strong private-property rights and weakened labor rights. As economic profit has been privatized and distributed among the few, debt has been communalized and pushed off to the many. Free markets and free trade are not equally accessible to all individuals, as neoliberal economic theory suggests, but instead favor the strong over the weak. These examples indicate that the premises of individualism—that people exist in isolation, and that economic success or misfortune is created in isolation—are not true. Individualism is the creed of the elite because it allows them to cover up the relationships that favor some and not others. The 1 percent want everyone to believe that success is self-made because this belief hides their debt to the community and allows them to blame all those who are less successful—the 99 percent. The creed of individualism is often padded with images of God residing at the top as a lonely individual, as well as images of isolated believers whose main concern is their individual salvation. This creed shapes not only the lives of the elites but also the lives of many who belong to the 99 percent, including the poorest of the poor, because many of them dream of becoming wealthy and powerful someday in the future.

Nevertheless, the creed of individualism does not benefit the multitude. Very few ever get the opportunity to "pull themselves up by their own bootstraps." The so-called American dream, promoting the idea that all individuals have the opportunity to move up the social ladder, rarely proves workable for the masses. When workers in the United States were better off, for instance, it was not because of individualism but because they had strong unions, which fought for eight-hour workdays, rest on weekends, pension plans, and various protections from exploitation. Likewise, when civil rights were granted in the history of the United States, whether voting rights for women and minorities or racial integration of public spaces, it was due to communal action rather than the creed of individualism or strong individual leaders. Not even some of the greatest individuals, such as Rev. Martin Luther King Jr. or Mohandas Gandhi, would have accomplished much on their own.

The multitude knows that individualism is a lie and that relationship is a fact of life, for better or worse. We owe everything to others, including the things that we take for granted, such as our ability to learn to speak a certain language and express ourselves so that others can understand. This is one of the basic insights of the Christian faith and of many other religions as well. Our lives are constituted by relationships, which include our relation with the divine as well as our relations with our parents and relatives, our teachers, and our friends. Moreover, our lives are also constituted by relationships with service providers, a global workforce, and our environments, and it is not always clear where one of these relationships ends and another begins, including our relationship with the divine.

The Jesus movement understood itself in terms of all these relationships, but Jesus was also aware of the tensions. It is these tensions that the creed of individualism overlooks as well. When the family as an institution turned into another kind of individualism because elite families who benefited from political and religious advantages turned against the many other families who did not enjoy such benefits, Jesus pronounced a challenge to the family. In the presence of his own mother and siblings, he refused to acknowledge the bonds of kinship and designed his movement to provide relationships that would ultimately prove to be more helpful: "Looking at those who sat around him, he said, 'Here are my mother and my brothers! Whoever does the will of my God is my brother and sister and mother'" (Mark 3:34–35). The notion of justice in the Bible is embedded in the affirmation and restoration of such relationships; it is not an abstract principle of fairness, personified by a blindfolded woman holding a pair of scales. Instead, justice is bringing those who have been treated unjustly back into the community while challenging those who have promoted injustice and curbing their transgressions. [16]

Many of the liberation traditions and theologies share such an understanding of relationship and justice, and today it is revived and revitalized in the Occupy movement. One way in which the Occupy movement gives expression to these relationships is through its understanding of class, which is at the core of the movement. Class, in this context, is presented not as the existence of independent strata in society—the most common definition in the United States today, if class is discussed at all—but as a matter of relationship between the classes. That the 1 percent and the 99 percent are deeply related is not a new insight for those who have experienced exploitation in more dramatic forms, but it is a fresh insight in the public discussions in the United States and other countries, which have been shaped by neoliberal capitalism.

Yet this fresh understanding of relationship is not without detractors. Even when it is pointed out, the relationship between the 1 percent and the 99 percent is frequently denied not only by conservatives but also by liberals. The conservatives blame the 99 percent, and especially those on the lower end of the 99 percent, for their misfortunes. The liberals may be more open to the discussion of class but tend to hold on to understandings of class as harmless stratifications. On the one hand, conservatives lay the burden on those who are less successful, exhorting them to work harder and to live more virtuous lives. Liberals, on the other hand, see the task as lifting less privileged people up into the next stratum through programs designed to create more level playing fields, such as education and other projects that will enable those whom they consider "less fortunate" to get ahead in life. In both cases the symbiotic relationship between the 1 percent and the 99 percent is not clearly grasped. The truth is that many members of the lower classes work harder than anyone else, often at several jobs at once, without getting ahead. People are "less fortunate" not by accident but because others benefit from their misfortune, and they have little choice but to work for lower wages and fewer benefits.

Many biblical traditions, and particularly Jesus's own proclamations in the Gospels, speak of relationships and forms of justice that reverse the social order. The parable of the unforgiving servant (Matt. 18:21–35), for instance, is not a moral tale that people should forgive others because they have been forgiven by God. It is a reminder that forgiveness of debt is a way of life that makes more sense for working people than the individualism of the wealthy and the masters. The servant whose debt has been forgiven by a very untypical master, who acts against the logic of all masters, is now free to forgive the much smaller debt of one of his fellow servants. This ability to forgive debt is where true wealth lies, as it creates stronger relationships and solidarity among the servants that are worth much more than petty sums of money. If the master changes his mind in the future and starts clamping down on the servants again, it is the relationship among the servants that will protect them and enable resistance.

Mainline theology either pays little attention to relationship or moralizes about it. When pastors talk about relationship from the pulpits, for instance, they often morally exhort people to be less individualistic, thereby perpetuating the myth that individualism is real. But many liberation theologies have recognized the reality of relationship for years. Womanist theologies, for instance, are aware that the lives and circumstances of black women are tied to those of black men, and to those of white men and women, and many others, for good or for ill. While unjust relationships along the lines of gender, race, and class are mostly invisible for those who benefit from them, those who feel the pressures in their own bodies are sorely aware of what is going on. Rather than being "special-interest theologies" for individual minorities, liberation theologies insist that we are always related and prophetically denounce the oppressive natures of many of our relationships.

The fact that we live in the complex intersections of race, class, gender, and sexuality should not be a cause of frustration, but a call to develop less oppressive and more productive relations. In order to develop these relations, theologians of various liberative traditions have at times had recourse to the ancient Christian doctrine of the Trinity.[17] The doctrine of the Trinity presents an image of the divine as multiplicity and the heart of the universe as relational and nonhierarchical. It speaks of the first and the second persons of the Trinity as sharing the same quality of being and intimately related to the Holy Spirit. The Cappadocian theologians of the fourth century used the term *perichoresis*, referring to the divine relationship of embrace and interpenetration, to describe this dynamic relation. In the beginning there is not one single God who then produces a Trinity; in the beginning there is a relationship that models the sort of unity in difference that is also characteristic of the multitude. There is no going back to some primordial unity without diversity.

While humans never know relationships that are completely devoid of pressures and distortions, relationships have a productive quality that can never be completely erased. Relationships are produced and can grow stronger even under the greatest of pressures, such as the solidarity of African Americans confronted with the harsh realities of slavery, the solidarity of women confronted with the pressures of unrelenting patriarchy, and the solidarity of workers confronted with ruthless exploitation in their workplaces. Hardt and Negri argue that today the metropolis is the place where great pressures are condensed in such a way that new solidarity emerges. For this reason, they consider the metropolis "one vast reservoir of common wealth."[18] The Occupy movement appears, to some extent, to prove them right.

Yet the multitude that is formed in these contexts is not without its problems, and it does not form spontaneously. The organic image of the body, which the apostle Paul adopts to describe the church as the body of Christ, helps us understand what is at stake. This image was originally promoted by the philosophers of the Roman Empire in order to remind the subjects of the empire that they are organically related, but in such a way that there can be no shifting of positions, resulting in an organic hierarchy. The feet can never dream of becoming the head and vice versa, but head and feet need each other. Neoliberal capitalism has forgotten even the wisdom of the Roman Empire, as it treats workers as expendable and of little consequence. Paul, however, turns this hierarchical image of the body upside down:

> The eye cannot say to the hand, "I have no need of you," nor again the head to the feet, "I have no need of you." On the contrary, the members of the body that seem to be weaker are indispensable, and those members of the body that we think less honorable we clothe with greater honor, and our less respectable members are treated with greater respect (1 Cor. 12:21–24).

This reversal is not primarily a pragmatic one, seeking to promote harmony within the body, but rather finds its justification in God's own rationale: "God has so arranged the body, giving the greater honor to the inferior member" (1 Cor. 12:24b).

As a result, the body of Christ models the multitude, where "if one member suffers, all suffer together with it," and "if one member is honored, all rejoice together with it" (1 Cor. 12:26). This kind of multitude requires work. It does not arise out of thin air, and it can always be coopted by the status quo. We agree with Hardt and Negri that the debate needs to be shifted from being the multitude to making the multitude: "The multitude is formed through articulations on the plane of immanence without hegemony."[19] This formation includes the formation of nature, rather than leaving behind nature, as capitalism does.[20]

The good news is that, as Hardt and Negri point out,

> the production of the common always involves a surplus that cannot be expropriated by capital or captured in the regimentation of the global political body. This surplus, at the most abstract philosophical level, is the basis on which

antagonism is transformed into revolt. Deprivation, in other words, may breed anger, indignation, and antagonism, but revolt arises only on the basis of wealth, that is, a surplus of intelligence, experience, knowledges, and desire.[21]

Here we can draw some parallels to our notion of a theological surplus, which emerges in the dialectical tension between immanence and transcendence, as will be discussed below. In other words, the status quo that is presented to us as the only reality does not have the last word: another world is possible.

One of the biggest challenges for the emerging relationships among the multitude is how to develop a broader and deeper form of solidarity. Well-meaning proponents of relationship and solidarity have often had to fight the blatant rejections of relationship and solidarity of the 1 percent. It is unfortunate that many middle-class and poor people echo the powerful when they reject other people out of hand, such as immigrants or lesbian, gay, bisexual, or transgender people. One way in which the proponents of relationship and solidarity have fought this battle is by proclaiming that we do not need to be afraid of other people, that others are humans too, and that "others are just like us." Parents often tell their children that others are just like us in order to reduce their fear of others. The problem with this approach, however, is that although it is preferable to the blatant rejection of others, it tends to turn other people into mirror images of one's own self, without recognizing them for who they are. The result is that others can still be misused for one's own purposes.

One of the criticisms leveled at the Occupy movement is that it is predominantly white and middle class and that there are relatively few minorities involved. But as we have shown, there have been efforts made to value and respect minority voices, for instance by giving them priority of speech in the general assemblies. In Dallas, for instance, different groups collaborated across differences, from established groups like Move-On and the unions to small art collectives and racial minority groups. This does not always happen in Texas, and it should be noted that the homeless were part of the movement too, and that a community of Hare Krishnas brought food every day. We should also add that involving the middle class in the Occupy movement is a more important accomplishment than it might seem at first sight, especially when the middle class begins to realize that it is not out there merely to help others but that it is itself deeply affected by the economic crisis and thus shares in some structures of oppression with the rest of the 99 percent. This is the first step toward what we are calling "deep solidarity."

The Occupy movement has, therefore, the opportunity to develop unity in diversity in powerful ways. One practical example is Occupy Homes, a branch of the Occupy movement, which started in Minneapolis and Atlanta. Cat Salonek, an organizer with Occupy Homes in Minneapolis, notes that this spin-off of the Occupy movement is aware of what she calls the "unchecked privilege on the plaza." Not everyone can afford to stay in tents for extended periods of time. Privilege is addressed in Occupy Homes as people meet face-to-face with families who are threatened by eviction and with people in struggling neighborhoods. People gather with a specific purpose—preventing foreclosure and eviction from a house—and these projects bring people together and keep growing as more foreclosures are addressed. As a result, whole neighborhoods are being organized. Occupy Homes also brings together different sectors of the Occupy movement, including a faith component, as some of the work is done and presented in roundtable discussions in churches.

As the 99 percent are beginning to understand their deep solidarity and thus their fundamental unity, how to deal with difference remains a fundamental issue. One reason is that difference has often been used by the 1 percent to divide and conquer the 99 percent. Differences of race, ethnicity, and gender have been used for the benefit of the system. When white landowners in seventeenth-century Virginia used the category of race to pit poor white people against black people, the poor white people gained some small privileges over their black peers. At the same time, they lost something much more essential—namely, their deep solidarity with black people, which would have put them in a much stronger position.[22] The same is true when men and women are pitted against each other in the workplace: men gain some privileges, often in terms of status and better pay, but they lose what really counts—the ability to organize together with women, so that all workers are better off in the end. In these examples, racism and sexism benefit the masters and the employers more than they benefit the workers.

Jewish Argentinean religion scholar Santiago Slabodsky is right when he reminds us that the racially privileged participants in the Occupy movement fail "to understand that historically they have been beneficiaries and not victims" of institutions like slavery.[23] As we remember the history of slavery, however, we also need to keep in mind that not all white Southerners benefited equally from slavery: the white owners of the Southern plantations benefited exponentially. According to Theodore W. Allen, "the poor and propertyless European-Americans were the principal element in the day-today enforcement of racial oppression," as even the poorest white man "could now find pride in his race."[24] The white landowners were thus more powerful and better off than ever, as the poor whites could be employed in the control of the African American slaves.

The awareness of class differences between the 1 percent and the 99 percent, which the Occupy movement promotes, helps us put the differences of race, ethnicity, gender, and sexuality in a broader context. In the words of Hardt and Negri, "The multitude is composed of radical differences, singularities, that can never be synthesized in an identity. The radicality of gender difference, for example, can be included in the biopolitical organization of social life, the life renovated by the multitude, only when every discipline of labor, affect, and power that makes gender difference into an index of hierarchy is destroyed."[25] Rather than pitting one form of difference against another—like race against class or class against gender—the lens of class helps us put these differences to constructive use.

The privileges in terms of class, gender, and race that some participants in the Occupy movement enjoy can now be put to work. Certain resources of the middle class (and even of the 1 percent), such as academic expertise, personal and professional connections, and financial resources, are useful for all members of the 99 percent. Instead of using their privileges to create power differentials, members of the middle class can use their knowledge, expertise, and connections to strengthen the movement. Similarly, white people can use their privileges in society as white allies in support of people of color and immigrants. A white Anglo-Saxon politician or pastor joining the cause of immigrants, for instance, could be extremely beneficial to the movement. In terms of gender and heterosexual privileges, the movement for justice can benefit from solidarity between men and women, and between heterosexual people and lesbian, gay, bisexual, and transgender people.

It is important to realize that privilege exists, but also that this sort of privilege is often not much more than the system "throwing a bone" to the privileged so that they will continue to toe the line: the middle class is hanging on to the false hope that they are more like the ruling class than the working class; members of the dominant race and ethnicities act out their whiteness, with the illusion that they are better off than and superior to the minorities; and males still have some advantages of pay over women, but they don't run the show just because they are male, as the janitors' union would remind us.

As lines are being redrawn and new connections made, we will also begin to see religious differences in a new light. Many Christians in the United States assume that there is a firm line between Christians and non-Christians. But the issue at hand is not whether people profess belief in God or not; the question is what kind of God and what kind of power they affirm. The theology of the multitude that we are developing here often finds itself in closer proximity with liberation theologians from other religions than with some Christian theologians who uphold dominant images of God. South African Islamic scholar Farid Esack, for instance, notes a preferential option for the oppressed in the Qur'an, which is rooted in the identification of God with the oppressed.[26] Esack observes that in some places "the Qur'an makes a clear choice for the *mustad'afun* [the marginalized and oppressed] against the *mustakbirun* [the arrogant and powerful] even though the former may not be Muslim."[27]

It is more important to ask how God's power manifests itself and in what direction power flows than to debate abstractly the existence of "God" in general. This awareness opens a new chapter in interreligious dialogue, as the conversations not only become richer and deeper but also allow for a better appreciation of both similarities and differences. Those who affirm power as a top-down process and those who see God or ultimate reality upholding it appear to be closer to each other—no matter whether they are Christian or not—than to those who affirm alternative forms of power that move from the bottom up. In this regard, Christians need to rethink completely what we say about God and community, as will be discussed in the following chapters.

IMMANENCE AND TRANSCENDENCE

According to conventional understandings, "immanence" refers to things that belong to this world and "transcendence" refers to things that go beyond it. The notion of transcendence is problematic for progressive thinkers because they seek to focus on the concerns of this world rather than on what is otherworldly. They are often suspicious of religion because they see it as concerned mostly with otherworldly transcendence. Postcolonial and cultural theorist Gayatri Chakravorty Spivak, for instance, says theology is foreign to her thinking, and she is wary of religious talk, which is often undergirded by the dichotomy of nature and supernature.[28] Hardt and Negri have written explicitly against transcendence: "The multitude, today, however, resides on the imperial surfaces where there is no God the Father and no transcendence. . . . The multitude has no reason to look outside its own history and its own present productive power for the means necessary to lead toward its constitution as a political subject."[29]

These thinkers' suspicion of anything that smacks of transcendence is understandable, considering how transcendence has been domesticated and coopted by religions and theologies of the status quo, whether liberal or conservative. Conservative theologies' teachings on creationism and intelligent design,[30] for instance, tend to identify transcendence with the way things are. This sort of transcendence frequently provides a sacred canopy protecting the hierarchies of power that sustain the status quo. But this happens even in liberal theologies, which seek to challenge the ways the conservative status quo has come to define religion. Liberal theologies' emphasis on human experience, all the way back to Friedrich Schleiermacher, often identifies transcendence with the status quo as well, especially where it endorses the value systems of the modern world. This approach becomes especially problematic when the adoption of theories of evolution turns into a widespread social Darwinism, which identifies the "survival of the fittest" with the elites. Yet the insistence on immanence can also be coopted to celebrate the status quo, as seen in German Protestantism of the nineteenth century and contemporary civil religion in the United States. In these examples, God is perceived as embodied in the dominant expressions of culture, religion, politics, and economics. That is why megachurches are so fashionable: they are seen as the embodiment of God on earth. We need a different approach.

Instead of pitting immanence and transcendence against each other, let us take another look at the potential of each term for an emerging theology of the multitude. At the heart of a theology of the multitude is a deep sense that things do not have to be the way they are now. This sense links multitude theology to the various liberation theologies and distinguishes it from any other type of theological or religious reflection that works on the grounds of the way things are. Here we can find new experiences of transcendence and immanence that are in diametrical opposition to theologies of the status quo.

In the history of theology, the notion of transcendence has often played an important role in theologies of resistance. Twentieth-century Swiss theologian Karl Barth is widely known for his emphasis on the otherness of God. This meant, for Barth, that God cannot be coopted by the status quo and by a church that merely supports the dominant political and economic powers.

However, what is often overlooked, even by many of those who claim to be Barthians at present, is that Barth's emphasis on God's otherness is deeply rooted in an understanding that things do not have to be as they are now.

This puts Barth's work in the camp of liberation traditions, as it has inspired liberation theologians like Gustavo Gutiérrez, James Cone, and Frederick Herzog. Moreover, Barth's sense of God's otherness was closely related to his encounter with blue-collar workers in the small Swiss town of Safenwil. There, Barth realized how closely God's transcendence had been identified with the elites in political and economic life in mainline churches and theologies, a problem that has plagued Christianity throughout its history and even today. Learning about the lives of the workers, their struggles and their pressures, Barth began to understand that the Christian understanding of God's transcendence had to be radically revised. Emphasizing that in the Jewish and Christian traditions God always sides with the oppressed and against the oppressors,[31] Barth not only revolutionized theology but also joined in the support of the unions and the Swiss Socialist party, of which he remained a member until the end of his life.[32] Theology and organizing were closely linked in the early days of Barth's theology.

In the midst of the struggles of everyday life, new understandings of transcendence have developed that are crucial to a theology of the multitude. Mark Lewis Taylor helpfully distinguishes among the transcendence of emancipatory politics, the transcendence of command in authoritarian systems, and the transcendence of ordering function in Western capitalism.[33] The latter two forms of transcendence support the status quo, one by endorsing the unchecked authority of elites from the outset, and the other by endorsing those who end up on top in the capitalist marketplace. All this throws new light on one of the core problems in the United States, where people's minds are so colonized by the status quo that it is hard for the multitude to identify radically different notions of transcendence. The only widely available notions of transcendence that display some criticism of the status quo are those of the doomsday prophets, and so it is no wonder that many Christians find it easier to believe that the world will go up in flames someday soon than that capitalism will ever end.

The notions of transcendence of theology of the multitude bear some resemblance to the kind of transcendence embodied in the incarnation, where God becomes human in Jesus Christ.[34] Since, as classical Christianity emphasizes, these two natures cannot be confused or separated (as expressed in the Council of Chalcedon in 451 CE), transcendence and immanence cannot be defined according to divinity and humanity. Both divinity and humanity are part of the transcendent, and both divinity and humanity are part of the immanent. This changes everything because transcendence is no longer that which hovers over the immanent, superior and at a safe distance. As Barth and many liberation theologians understood, the story of Jesus Christ being born in lowly conditions redefines our understanding of God's transcendence. Transcendence is not that which is opposed to immanence in general, but it is an alternative form of immanence that challenges the immanence of the status quo.

Any notion of transcendence that fails to understand this reversal is bound to end up endorsing another hierarchy and thus other forms of oppression. The work of John Milbank, one of the founders of so-called radical orthodoxy, provides an example of this problem. He encourages "a new postliberal participatory democracy that is enabled by the aristocracy of an education that seeks after the common good and absolute transcendent truth. Finally, we need to see that it is equally enabled by a monarchic principle that permits a unified power at the limit to intervene in the name of . . . equity."[35] This is the sort of transcendence that Hardt and Negri oppose for good reasons. Not only does it perpetuate unchecked hierarchies, but it also neglects any sense of the agency of the multitude, which is key to a theology of the multitude.[36] Hardt and Negri's suspicion that "transcendent sovereignty" today is tied to the "transcendental power of the republic of property"[37] should give us pause, both because it unmasks relations that often remain invisible and because it describes the forces that are responsible for holding the multitude in check, even if they operate with the best of intentions.

Alternative images of transcendence throw new light on the agency of the multitude. Jesus Christ demonstrates this alternative agency in his own life by rejecting the top-down agency of the Roman Empire that appears in the form of the devil's offer to grant Jesus power over all the kingdoms of the world (Matt. 4:8–10) and in Jesus's promotion and embodiment of another way of life: "Blessed are you who are poor, for yours is the kingdom of God" (Luke 6:20), and "But woe to you who are rich, for you have received your consolation" (Luke 6:24). The agency that counts in the kingdom of God, which is "among you" (Luke 17:21), is not the agency of the rich; it is the agency of the poor. This kingdom is therefore better grasped as an anti-kingdom, as the reign of God is unlike the reigns of the powerful of this world.

Without referencing Jesus, Hardt and Negri grasp something of this alternative agency when they talk about the prophetic capacity of "the poor": "Only the poor lives radically the actual and present being, in destitution and suffering, and thus only the poor has the ability to renew being."[38] Nevertheless, it does not seem necessary to us to declare "the poor" to be "god on earth,"[39] as Hardt and Negri do. While there is good reason to point out the family resemblance between the agency of the multitude and the divine—Jesus himself does so repeatedly—the place of transcendence itself is better left open. This signals the limits and shortcomings of all that we do, and the fact that the anti-kingdom, or the reign of God, is not yet established in its entirety.

It is not necessary for a theology of the multitude to identify the transcendent qualities of the multitude—a multitude that embodies a surplus of insight and energy that those who are identified with the status quo generally lack—with the transcendent as such or with God.[40] This is the wisdom of the Second Commandment, which prohibits making and worshiping images of God (Exod. 20:4). Keeping the place of the transcendent open reminds us that we are still on the road and do not have a permanent dwelling place where the status quo rules supreme: "For here we have no lasting city, but we are looking for the city that is to come," states a famous passage in Hebrews 13:14. This sort of open transcendence does not have to be understood in otherworldly terms. Jesus's own message about the difference the reign of God makes in this world displays a similar restlessness: "Foxes have holes, and birds of the air have nests; but the Son of Man has nowhere to lay his head" (Matt. 8:20). These insights, we believe, are shared by the Occupy movement and symbolized by dwelling in tents on public property.

In this regard, the heart of the theology of the multitude is not religion in general but an experience of otherness and transcendence, which can be mediated through religion as well as through other experiences. The problem with mainline religion, as we see it today, is that it often fights experiences of otherness and transcendence as openness, and it does so in the name of a transcendence that backs up the status quo. This happens, for instance, when mainline religion promotes images of God as a monarch in the sky whose main concern is eternal salvation in heaven, images that are then pitted against images of God at work in the common people or in grassroots movements that seek to make a difference here and now. A similar rejection of experiences of otherness and transcendence can be found in the current form of party politics in the United States, which tends to be unsatisfactory for a theology of the multitude not because it is politics but because it lacks this moment of otherness and transcendence as openness. Politics and religion are not fundamentally opposed in many of our traditions—the idea that they can be separated is a modern misconception. The better question is what our politics will be. For those who, like us, remain committed to matters of religion, this means that we can no longer accept definitions of religion that keep it safely in check so that it cannot challenge the political, economic, and cultural status quo.

In conclusion, a theology of the multitude offers a new perspective not only on transcendence but also on immanence. Immanence is changed in the encounter with transcendence in the sense that it becomes a space that provides both resistance and new opportunities for the multitude to become genuinely productive. Immanence is the new world—the anti-kingdom, or the reign of God—growing in the midst of the old. Understood in this way, both immanence and transcendence have a specific horizon: overcoming a status quo that does not allow alternatives and that exploits the agency and productivity of the multitude. An interesting parallel of a critique of a particular status quo that harnesses the agency and productivity of the multitude for its own gain can be found in the prophet Samuel's warnings that the establishment of a kingship in Israel means that "the king who will reign over you" will "take your sons and appoint them to his chariots and to be his horsemen, and to run before his chariots," and "he will take your daughters to be perfumers and cooks and bakers" (1 Samuel 8:11, 8:13).

DISTRIBUTION AND PRODUCTION

Theologies concerned with justice issues have long been interested in matters of fairness in how wealth is distributed. Here, the focus is on the remission of debt, the sharing of resources, and the giving and receiving of gifts so that all have enough to live. Yet there is another aspect that is frequently overlooked: the aspect of production. While distribution is indeed a major problem as the rich get richer and the poor get poorer, the deeper problem has to do with production. The crucial question is how the productive capacities of people are valued, as there are billions of people who work around the clock, often at several jobs, but still live in poverty. A further question is whether people are in positions where they can employ their productive and creative capacities so that their community as a whole benefits.[41]

What does a focus on production have to do with theology? Even though theology has often contributed to the passivity of the people because many people rely on the clergy and theologians to tell them what to believe and because their participation in religious activities does not encourage agency, a theology of the multitude promotes a different image. A theology of the multitude understands that many of our traditions encourage agency and productivity. Worship, for instance, has nothing to do with passive reception or narrow religious ritual. Worship, as the prophet Isaiah points out, has to do with the production of justice (Isa. 58: 5–7). We will come back to this idea in chapter 6. The various feedings of the four thousand and of the five thousand (Mark 8:1–10; Matt. 14:13–21) in the Gospels are not just a witness to the miraculous powers of Jesus; they can also be understood as testimonies of the agency and resourcefulness of the multitude in taking care of each other. Jesus's healings tend to encourage agency and productivity as well. He responds to a man who has been waiting for help for thirty-eight years with these words: "Stand up, take your mat and walk" (John 5:8).

The productivity of the multitude does not require a rejection of diversity, but rather a concern for the flourishing of the community. Hardt and Negri make an important distinction between the crowd, the masses, the rabble, or the mob—all social bodies that must be led by strong individuals—and the multitude. The multitude "designates an active social subject, which acts on the basis of what the singularities share in common. The multitude is an internally different multiple social subject whose constitution and action is based not on identity or unity (or, much less, indifference) but on what it has in common."[42] In other words, the multitude is tied together not by its uniformity or inherent similarities, but rather by collaboration in common projects that benefit all.

This is why the apostle Paul could celebrate the emerging freedom of the community without having to worry about uniformity: "But now that faith has come we are no longer subject to a disciplinarian, for in Christ Jesus you are all children of God through faith. As many of you as were baptized into Christ have clothed yourselves with Christ. There is no longer Jew or Greek, there is no longer slave or free, there is no longer male and female; for all of you are one in Christ Jesus" (Gal. 3:25–28). As the structures that exploit diversity for the purpose of domination are dismantled, productivity for the sake of the common good is set free. The different identities are not erased but transformed: as men swear off patriarchy, slave masters swear off gain from slaveholding, and dominant races and ethnicities loosen their grip, new collaborations become possible.

It is crucial to keep in mind that the dominated voices are not folded into the dominant majority. Their distinctiveness is not erased as they become part of the multitude. On the contrary, the formerly dominated voices make substantial and productive contributions to the community. When members of the Occupy movement claim their status as the multitude by stating, "We are the 99 percent," they claim not only a fairer distribution of resources for all but also their own agency, and they point to the productive contributions that they are making to the community. This is often overlooked in a society that celebrates and rewards the ones in positions of power and privilege—the "first" rather than the "last." The Gospel message turns this around in a statement that appears to be deeply sympathetic to the concerns of the 99 percent: "Many who are first will be last, and the last will be first" (Matt. 19:30, 20:16).

Subverting the idea of a monarchy, where there is only one strong ruler who makes the decisions (the "decider," a term coined by former president George W. Bush), Jesus makes the following announcement to his disciples—those "who have left everything and followed [him]": "Truly I tell you, at the renewal of all things, when the Son of Man is seated on the throne of his glory, you who have followed me will also sit on twelve thrones, judging the twelve tribes of Israel" (Matt. 19:27–28). Not only is monarchy subverted here, as there is more than one throne, but the criteria of judgment are also reversed, as the last will be first and the first will be last. This is no top-down monarchy, where production is organized from the top, nor is it a democracy where the elite citizens hold the reins of production. This is what might be called a *laocracy* or *ochlocracy* that is built on the productivity of the multitude, which is now dutifully acknowledged and valued by people who are their peers.

The multitude is, therefore, anything but another service project. This is news for a church and a society that has structured its relations with the "least of these" in the form of service projects, whether they take the shape of charity or of advocacy. The traditional terms of "following Jesus" or "discipleship" do not refer to involvement in service projects; rather, these terms refer to joining in solidarity with the least of these and acknowledging and reinforcing their agency. In short, discipleship means becoming a productive agent in relationship with other productive agents. This is what we are calling "deep solidarity." Where in the past solidarity, even for progressive Christians, often meant a decision of the will to be in support of the "least of these," solidarity now begins with an understanding that we are all in the same boat: we are the 99 percent, and we challenge the 1 percent to stop building their power and wealth at our expense and invite them to join us. Solidarity continues with celebrating a common productivity that has always been at work—otherwise, little would get done in the world—but that the system has concealed from us. This common productivity has been covered up by putting people in competitive relationships. Yet real competition is not primarily located where we usually look for it: in the relations between the races, men and women, and the working class and middle class. Real competition is located in the relations between the 1 percent and the 99 percent, whereby the 1 percent becomes wealthier and more powerful all the time and everybody else is increasingly subjected to austerity measures.

To be sure, the agency and productivity developed here can take many different forms. All forms of agency and productivity that contribute to the well-being of the community rather than to private interests alone are welcome. This means that we need to draw a line between the agency of the multitude and the arrogant, top-down agency of control that is embodied by the 1 percent; we also need to expose the claims of the 1 percent, shored up by neoliberal economic theory, that if the rich are doing better, everyone is doing better. The agency that has been demonstrated by women, minorities, and organized workers is instructive because it is an agency that develops under conditions of adversity, without efforts to achieve top-down dominance.

Would it be possible that the multitude, after gaining power, would behave like the 1 percent? That the multitude is after a simple reversal—so that they would be the masters and the 1 percent the slaves—is an often-repeated suspicion, but how would this be possible? How could the multitude ever take unilateral, top-down action if it is leaderless—or "leaderfull" (see chapter 3)—to such a degree that there are millions of leaders? Even a call for a "dictatorship" of the proletariat could only amount to a reversal of the term "dictatorship," as the lordship of Christ is a reversal of the lordship of the Roman emperor. Jesus's rejection of top-down power, embracing the power of weakness to which Paul testifies, models another way of being productive. In 2 Corinthians, Paul hears Jesus say to him, "My grace is sufficient for you, for power is made perfect in weakness" (12:9). By the same token, a truly *laocratic* or *ochlocratic* situation can only present power being made perfect in weakness and rules out dictatorial rule of any form. The form of power at work among the multitude is in stark contrast with the power of the status quo.

Hardt and Negri describe the agency and productivity of the multitude in terms of love—a term that matches Christian imagery. But we need to be clear how this concept of love differs from what we usually mean by this term. The love of the multitude differs, for instance, from the love that is expressed by the modern concept of bourgeois love, which is often privatized and self-serving. Here, love is reserved for family and an exclusive circle of friends, as well as the production of heterosexual couples, which has been the theme of thousands of Hollywood movies over the years. According to Hardt and Negri, the love of the multitude is not self-serving but open to the community, as "love means precisely that our expansive encounters and continuous collaborations bring us joy."[43] Love is realized through agency and production, which constructs and reconstructs self and other and their relationship with the community; it has nothing to do with being starry-eyed or mesmerized by another person.[44]

Yet there are limits to the notion of love, even where it seeks the common good. In contemporary theologies of various affiliations, there has been a distinction between the powers of coercion and attraction, initially developed in the theology of Friedrich Schleiermacher.[45] Many liberals tend to envision love in terms of attraction and perhaps the related soft powers of persuasion. What is commonly overlooked, however, is that even this sort of love can be used in the service of the powers that be. In globalizing capitalism, for instance, the soft power of attraction is far more effective and seductive than the hard power of the military. In other words, this sort of love is good for business, as it facilitates the flow of power from the top down. The advertising industry, for instance, accomplishes more when it works through attraction and love, and cultural dominance often works along those lines as well. The American movie industry, for instance, has been much more effective in spreading goodwill for neoliberal capitalism than any military action could ever hope to be.

For these reasons, the notion of love needs to be tempered with the notion of justice. This insight is deeply embedded in Jewish and Christian theology. If justice, as we said above, is about restoring relationship, it includes rejecting and deconstructing that which inhibits this process. Love tempered by justice can take the form of tough love, which is not coercion or violence but rather a form of love that enables us to draw clear lines when it comes to oppressive relationships. When the 99 percent stand up to the 1 percent, this is not only a matter of claiming justice but also a deep expression of love. As Jürgen Moltmann has observed, the ancient biblical hope for the judgment of oppressors, which effectively puts an end to oppressive relationships, is part of what truly gives hope to the oppressed.[46] This means that God's own love can be expressed in terms of justice. Justice, like love, is not a narrow principle but the basis of the common life of the multitude and part of the joy that it experiences.

While productivity rather than mere distribution and redistribution is at the heart of a theology of the multitude, it is important to bear in mind that no clear-cut action plan can be put forth. Such a clear-cut action plan would require once again the forms of top-down power that belong to the old eon rather than the new. The Occupy movement in its early days embodied this insight: it chose to be a leaderless movement, as those who operated in leadership roles resisted the temptation to claim authority for their own personal benefit. Strands of the earliest Christian theologies, which the apostle Paul quotes in Philippians, say something similar about Christ: "Though he was in the form of God, [he] did not regard equality with God as something to be exploited, but emptied himself" (2:6–7). It seems to us that these new ways of life are teaching us something about the "form of God" as well: emptying oneself of top-down power and reclaiming other sorts of power may be more God-like than we had ever suspected.

The disadvantage of such leaderless movements is that they allow for no quick resolutions and fixes, and they reduce the expectation of efficiency, which is so deeply engrained in the mentality of capitalism. Nevertheless, a slower process of addressing and resolving the problems of the world and an efficiency that rests on the shoulders of many may be more effective in the long run. Another advantage of a leaderless movement is that it cannot be destroyed easily, as the destruction of those whom the system identifies as leaders will not bring the movement to a halt.

What happens when people discover that both their own powers and God's power are different than what mainline Christianity, whether conservative or liberal, has told them? Without this awareness of how the power that is at the heart of the universe is different, people will continue to bend to the pressures exerted by the wealthy and the powerful. Being told in many ways that God is on the side of those who are on top, or simply living with the tacit assumption that this is the way things are, people are kept in darkness about their own power to make a difference. After all, most of our images of God portray the divine as located on the top. At present, these values are embodied most clearly by right-wing politics and religion, but even liberals tend to follow suit, as they rarely provide alternatives, and simply placing God somewhere in the middle does not help much. The Occupy movement may help the multitude to change their minds on these matters.

Finally, we need to note that asserting the agency and productivity of the multitude will not go without conflict, a conflict more intense than what we have already seen in discussions about distribution. The efforts to nullify the power of the multitude are many, and it is striking that, as Hardt and Negri observe, so many of these efforts are tied up with Christian theology and doctrine.[47] Here, the false transcendence that we discussed above may be the biggest challenge. Those who see the power of God at the top, intimately linked with all the other powers found at the top, feel obligated to fight the multitude. While there is little agreement among churches and theologians today, there is a common mood of rejection directed against liberative theologies, to which theologies of the multitude belong, that assert new images of God and new ways of life. So the multitude continues to be opposed not only by those at the top whose wealth and power keeps growing at the expense of the multitude, but also by all those who feel that this is the way it should be. For this reason, the forces that seek to defeat the new paradigm often come from within, just as Judas betrayed Jesus. Nevertheless, the good news is that history does not belong to the Judases, nor does it belong to the Roman Empire or any other empire that has risen and fallen throughout history.

Chapter Five

Reimagining the God of the Multitude

We soon painfully discover, however, that not all of us have the same mind
when we use the word God.
—Frederick Herzog, *God-Walk: Liberation Shaping Dogmatics* [1]

Participation in the Occupy movement prompted many people to rethink
their images of God and their relationship with the divine. The question is
whether dominant images of God speak to what they were experiencing in
the movement. For protest chaplain Jennifer Wilder, God is "the love and
connection that we share among ourselves. God is commitment to collectiv-
ity." [2] The Rev. Stephanie Shockley says her involvement has changed her
understanding of Jesus. She now understands Jesus and his followers in a
more personal way. Jesus is now more real to her. Jesus is an actual person
who walks and lives among us and becomes very present. This has implications for how we understand both humanity and divinity. [3]

The participation of clergy and protest chaplains and the carrying of
religious symbols and celebration of rituals on the streets with the Occupy
movement produced powerful responses and dynamics, especially in a culture where many people rarely experience religious support for progressive
causes. In our current cultural climate, religious symbols are heavily identified with conservative agendas. For the most part, God is claimed either by
the right wing or by the status quo. What is odd, however, is that this trend
does not match many of the basic images of our religious traditions. It is not
hard to see, for instance, where Jesus was found in the days of old: he lived in
deep solidarity not with the elites of his time but with the multitude, particularly with those who struggled with life, including the sick, social outcasts,

83

strong women of "dubious" reputation, and working people like fishermen, service workers, and agricultural workers. Being raised as a carpenter, he would have been in intimate contact with the many unemployed of his time, who regularly experienced layoffs after each of the larger jobs was completed.[4] And it is quite possible that Jesus experienced the pressures of unemployment or underemployment in his own life. He certainly was aware of the struggles that common people faced every day, which easily escaped those at the top and rarely showed up in conservative agendas (Matt. 20:1–16: the parable of the workers in the vineyard).

Not only did Jesus not support the conservative agendas of the elites of his day, but he also actively resisted them. He challenged religious legalism by healing on the Sabbath, putting the demands of liberation above the law: "Ought not this woman, a daughter of Abraham whom Satan bound for eighteen long years, be set free from this bondage on the sabbath day?" (Luke 13:16; for another healing on the Sabbath, see Mark 3:1–6). He challenged the myriad uses of religion that keep struggling people down (in John 9:2, the disciples wonder whether a man's sin or the sin of his parents caused the man to be born blind; in Matthew 23:4, Jesus notes that certain religious officials "tie up heavy burdens, hard to bear, and lay them on the shoulders of others"). He challenged the conservative pattern of marginalizing women and children (in John 4:27, the disciples are taken aback that Jesus is speaking with a woman; in Mark 10:13, the disciples try to prevent people from bringing their children—the insignificant ones of ancient societies—to Jesus). Jesus also challenged narrow notions of the family—at the core of conservative politics even today—by declaring that the true bonds that tie communities together are not biological and genetic but social: "Whoever does the will of God is my brother and sister and mother" (Mark 3:35) and "Whoever loves father or mother more than me is not worthy of me; and whoever loves son or daughter more than me is not worthy of me" (Matt. 10:37). In sum, the conservative worship of the status quo has no place in Jesus's life. He challenged the temple, the highest symbol of his religion (Mark 13:1–3); he refused to observe simple customs—like the washing of hands before eating—in order to make a point (Mark 7:1–23); he supported the causes of day laborers (Matt. 18:23–34, 20:1–16); he challenged the rich, saying, "It is easier for a camel to go through the eye of a needle than for someone who is rich to enter the kingdom of God" (Mark 20:25); and he even called into question private property (Mark 10:17–22; see also Luke

14:33). The early Christians must have understood him better, as they managed to live out some of these challenges, forming alternative communities and ways of life (Acts 2:43–47, 4:32–37).

GOD AT WORK

For believers, the challenge is bigger than religious symbols and images and their mostly conservative uses. The challenge for the future of any faith in God is whether its religious symbols and images point to the reality of God or not. If they do not point to the reality of God, even the most popular and commonly used symbols and images will ultimately collapse and disappear. This is what has happened to empire religion for centuries, and we suspect that it is about to happen again as the tide appears to be changing. Is it any wonder that young people in the United States are less committed to religion than their parents? The deep suspicion of religion in Europe that has always puzzled Americans is in part related to a long history of religion in support of the status quo, including widespread religious support of fascism and the German Third Reich. Unfortunately, many opportunities to reshape on a broader basis religious symbols and images in ways that would point more adequately to the reality of God were missed in Europe; perhaps we can do better this time, and it looks as if the Occupy movement might help us in this pursuit. It is because distorted images of God are so widespread in our own time that we have no choice but to reimagine the divine.

Rather than merely asking, "What would Jesus do?"—a slogan that has been marketed well by the WWJD movement—Christians might want to ask a more challenging question: "What is Jesus doing?" If the question is put like this, maintaining common conservative images of Jesus is more difficult, as the praxis of Jesus needs to be taken into account. Why would the Jesus who walked with the people on the dusty roads of Galilee and organized them have retired to sitting in church buildings or other places that are removed from where the action is? In the stories of the Gospels, Jesus spent considerably more time on the road than in the synagogue or the temple; he spent time walking through fields gleaning food or engaging in public debates in villages and cities, and he was on his way to the capital when he mocked the Roman governor by entering the city on the back of a donkey instead of a horse (Matt. 21:1–11). Where is Jesus walking now? Jesus spent time contemplating, but he spent even more time healing the colonized and their diseases, including the paralyzed, whose agency had been shattered, and the possessed, whose personalities had been destroyed. He combated religious neuroses by proclaiming the forgiveness of God and put people back on the road: "Stand up and take your bed and walk" (Mark 2:9) and "Get up!" (Mark 5:41). Are there parallels to those who are rising up and walking on Wall Street and in many of our cities? In his famous response to John the Baptist, Jesus pointed to what he was doing—healing and organizing for liberation ("The poor have good news brought to them")—rather than to the common emphasis of conservative theology on affirming abstract theological concepts or rejecting them, as liberals are tempted to do (see Matt. 11:2–6).

A related question that is bigger than Christianity is "Where is God at work?" This question has often been raised by those involved in liberation movements. It was one of the key questions for Dietrich Bonhoeffer, who as a Christian joined the resistance movement against Nazi Germany and another resistance movement that fought the majority of mainline churches that supported it. [5] In more recent decades, this question was also raised by budding forms of North American liberation theology that have now been forgotten or repressed because they could not be easily assimilated. Frederick Herzog, a liberation theologian who taught in the U.S. South, talked about *theopraxis*—the work of God—in order to identify the deep roots of our own actions (*orthopraxis*) that are the mark of liberation movements. [6] This question is crucial in those situations where activism is dominated by the privileged who enjoy being in control—whether staunch conservatives or well-meaning liberals. Examining the actions of God in resistance to the status quo can help us broaden our sense of which actions really matter in the struggle for liberation.

The greatest challenge for people of faith from the Occupy movement, therefore, is the question of where we find God at work. To be sure, this is not an idealistic question that can be addressed exclusively in light of the pious ideas that are found in people's minds or in the minds of religions communities. We agree with the bumper sticker that reads, "Don't believe everything you think." Rather, the question of where God is at work needs to be determined as our ideas push up against the stark pressures of life in which we are confronted with matters of life and death. This was the experience of the biblical character of Job: in the midst of great struggles and suffering, when the traditional and time-honored theological ideas presented by his friends crashed and burned, Job's encounter with God at the end of the book provides the ground for reimagining God and building a new way of life (Job 42:5). Mountaintop experiences are less helpful at this juncture.

If our response to where God is at work is "Nowhere in particular," then let us stop bothering with the God question right here and now. Why keep thinking about something that cannot be grasped? The more common response, of course, is that God is at work everywhere, which often turns out to mean that God is at work particularly with those who are powerful and successful, as they are usually seen as more blessed. Another common response is that God is at work primarily in the hallowed sanctuaries of religious worship, so people go to church in order to meet God there. In all of these examples, history shows that God can easily be made to fit our schemes so that business can continue as usual. However, if the response to the question of where God is at work is "with the least of these" (Matt. 25:45), "with people who are struggling with hunger and oppression" (Luke 1:46–55), on "the main streets" (Matt. 22:9), in the "streets and lanes of the town where the poor are gathered" (Luke 14:21), or with the uneducated, the powerless, and the lower classes (1 Cor. 1:26–29)—all places where deep solidarity is experienced—then it may be worth paying attention to religion and theology once again.

Unfortunately, many religious communities have given up asking questions about where God is at work. For the most part, they assume they know the answer: God is at work on the side of the status quo—which ultimately comes to mean that God *is* the status quo. While it is expected that pastors, theologians, and other religious officials will talk about God when they preach or teach and say something that is not too offensive or challenging to anyone, how many church committees wonder what God might be doing? In many ecclesial meetings that we have attended over the years in our denominations, it seemed to be taken for granted that theological debates are unnecessary because of a shared assumption that God is doing whatever we perceive the church to be doing.

Encountering God's agency in the context of the Occupy movement pushes us beyond the churches' self-centeredness. Nevertheless, this does not mean that we have to identify God with all that is going on, or else we would put the Occupy movement in the place of God. The challenge before us is less ambitious but therefore more interesting: we need to reflect on commonly held religious symbols and images of God and test them in real-life struggles. Rather than claiming command of the subject of God, a theology of the multitude finds itself in the place of the first disciples of Jesus, who walked with Jesus for extended amounts of time, often with more questions than answers, continuing to learn along the way.

ATHEISM HAS A POINT

Although many religious people hate to admit it, atheism has a point. Images of an all-powerful supreme being who controls everything from the top down, and who is also impassible and immutable, are laden with problems. There are the classical tensions between a God who can be omnipotent or omnibenevolent but not both at the same time. A God who is all-powerful and can do anything but who does not use this power to curb suffering and evil raises questions in terms of benevolence. Can we really think of such a God as being entirely benevolent? A God who is absolutely benevolent but who does nothing to curb suffering and evil raises questions in terms of the power to accomplish divine objectives. Can we really think of such a God as being all-powerful? We don't feel that these questions are of much help, as they work with notions of power and benevolence that are defined by dominant perspectives. What if God's power, for instance, is not the dominant power of absolute top-down control or the arbitrary power of tyrants, who claim the power to do whatever they want? What if God's benevolence is different from the benevolence of parents who spoil their children in order to keep them dependent?

The deepest problem of our most common images of God, supported by conservatives and liberals alike, is that images of the divine as omnipotent, impassible, and immutable tend to mirror the dominant powers that be, from ancient emperors to modern CEOs. No wonder people talk about God also as the "guy in the sky" or the "man upstairs." It is no accident that the latter of these expressions is applied both to God and the boss. Moreover, these images are not merely descriptive of the divine but are also used to increase power at the top of society and to restrict any other kind of power that might arise from other sectors. Such images of God are in the back of our minds when the alternative power of the Occupy movement is met with the dominant power of the police, who have repeatedly used excessive violence against peaceful protestors and even the elderly.[7] This connection of God and the dominant powers is no mere coincidence, it seems to us. It has to be produced and reproduced, as it does not follow naturally from many of the

Jewish and Christian traditions. There, God is most commonly portrayed in opposition to the dominant powers, including the Egyptian pharaohs and the rulers of other ancient empires in Babylonia, Mesopotamia, Assyria, and Persia; God is even portrayed in opposition to the institution of kingship in Israel and Judah, whose establishment has its roots in efforts to copy the power at work in the empires of the day (see Samuel 8:1–22).

Calling into question top-down images of God is, therefore, not just a concern for those who refuse to believe in God but also a concern for Jews and Christians who seek to be truly faithful to the God of their traditions. Responsible forms of atheism often match the concerns of people of faith, it is important to note, as they are not rants against the divine in general. Responsible forms of atheism are responses to particular forms of theism. Many theisms are headed in the wrong direction. This is true for more than simply those theisms that identify God and dominant power. Even those who argue that God is "something than which nothing greater can be thought," according to Anselm of Canterbury's famous definition,[8] fall into this trap because this definition affirms by default that which is considered to be "great" in the hierarchy of the world. It is not surprising, therefore, that Christianity itself shares closer links with some forms of atheism than is commonly noted. In many cases, Christians have more in common with certain forms of atheism than with certain forms of theism.

For good reasons, the early Christians themselves were considered atheists by the Romans. This was no mistake. While the Romans were religiously tolerant and happy to acknowledge and worship other divinities—even the Egyptian deities Isis and Osiris found their way into the Roman pantheon— they realized that the God worshiped by the Christians did not match their image of what a divinity should look like. And while the Romans, unlike the Jews, had no difficulty declaring that a human being could be divine, they were never able to accept the Christians' claim of Jesus's divinity. A crucified God—rejected by the Jewish religious establishment and executed by the Roman Empire as politically dangerous—was simply inconceivable.

The dominant theism of the Roman Empire was closely linked to classical theistic images of God as omnipotent, immutable, and impassible. Omnipotence is defined by Greek philosophical images, like Aristotle's notion of the first unmoved mover, whose power can only be considered absolute if there is nothing else that is able to influence it. Impassibility and immutability are, therefore, requirements of omnipotence because omnipotence is only that which cannot be affected by anything else, and which therefore cannot suffer or change. Suffering and changing imply a reduction of absolute power. Only human beings like the Roman emperors, who were imagined as close as possible to being omnipotent, immutable, and impassible, could therefore be declared divine. Conversely, it would be utter blasphemy to consider as divine human beings like Jesus Christ who rejected top-down power in favor of grassroots power, who were passionately engaged not with the elites but with the multitude, and who were able to change when the situation required it. While Jesus's alternative power and passion are better known, his willingness to change his mind is equally impressive (see Mark 7:24–30, the challenge of the Syrophoenician woman).

By claiming the divinity of Jesus Christ, the early Christians deconstructed commonly accepted notions of divinity. As a result, they put themselves in direct contradiction with the classical forms of theism that were upheld by the Roman Empire and most subsequent empires. This is the crucial move of early Christianity and its special contribution, even though a large number of Christians today and many Christians throughout history have not understood what this means: by declaring Jesus to be divine, Christians refused dominant notions of divinity and proposed an alternative. They did not simply claim a different divinity; they also opened up the way for rethinking the whole concept of divinity.

Religious pluralism as such does not necessarily help the project of a theology of the multitude. Our project is not reconciling different notions of divinity, whatever they may be, but reimagining divinity in all religions. The line that separates dominant and alternative images of God runs through the religions themselves. When the early Christians proclaimed that Jesus was Lord, they did not mean that Jesus was Lord over heavenly things alone, leaving the emperor's lordship over earthly things untouched. Saying that Jesus was Lord implied that the Roman emperor was not, and neither were any of the gods that supported the Roman Empire.[9] Religion before modernity was not accustomed to separating religion and politics as we do today. This is why ancient Jews listening to Jesus could not have understood that his advice to give God what is God's and the emperor what is the emperor's (Mark 12:17) meant giving to God what pertains to religion and giving everything else to the emperor. Giving to God what belongs to God meant to give everything to God. Of course, these early Christians did not fool themselves: they understood that the emperor was still enormously powerful, but they believed and declared that a different sort of power was at work at the heart of the universe.

Just as Jesus rejected the temptation to acquire the position of top-down power over the world offered to him by the devil (Matt. 4:8–11), the early Christians rejected the temptations of top-down power. A clash between different images of God and power was inevitable—the sort of clash that has surfaced again today with the Occupy movement. Where God is associated with the 1 percent, whether openly or by default, any refusal to identify God in this way is not a harmless theological dispute but will result in a clash and the sorts of persecutions with which we are familiar: Christians being fed to the wild animals in the Circus Maximus in Rome, dissenters burned at the stake in the medieval period, and prophets like the Rev. Martin Luther King Jr. being shot to death. Today's theologians of the multitude should not be surprised when they experience pushback as well.

The early Christians had a strong sense that Jesus Christ, whom they considered both human and divine, was no supreme being operating from the top down—omnipotent, immutable, and impassible. Their memories of Jesus Christ, and the difference that he made in people's lives in the midst of a world of empire, gradually helped them rethink divinity and who God is. While they came to believe that Jesus Christ was involved in the beginning of the world and creation, as the Gospel of John asserts, they also asserted that this Jesus Christ had become flesh (John 1:14) in a very particular form: Jesus Christ became flesh in solidarity with the multitude rather than with the dominant powers in religion, politics, and economics. In this way, the early Christians were able to reclaim ancient Jewish traditions that saw God at work not on the side of empires and the powerful but rather on the side of the people. Jesus's repeated claim that "the poor have good news brought to them" (Matt. 11:5 and Luke 4:18, echoing Isa. 61:1, "good news to the oppressed") resonates with an entirely different image of the divine, as one who "lived among us" (John 1:14).

These tensions between dominant imperial images of God and alternative images of God have followed Christianity ever since its earliest beginnings, and this is the reason why we now need to take another look at how the Occupy movement might help us rethink not only ourselves and the world but also the divine. This changes everything, both the big picture and our entire way of life, including common everyday religious practices such as prayer. Religious people often forget that there is no real communication with a God who is immutable and impassible because such a God is by definition not touched by anything but the concern for the maintenance of absolute power.

THE LIBERATION OF GOD FROM THEISM

Top-down images of God have been promoted by the theisms of the 1 percent through the ages. Yet the problem is bigger than the 1 percent, as top-down theism appears to be the default position, at work whenever generic notions of God are in circulation. Top-down theism is so pervasive that many people are not even aware that alternatives exist, despite many time-honored religious traditions that might teach us otherwise.

When children talk about God, for instance, they often envision God as an old man with a white beard sitting on a throne. This is one of the default images of God that is so widespread in many of our cultures that no one needs to teach it. We have found it ingrained in our own children's minds even though we know that it was never explicitly taught to them in Sunday school or by anyone else in particular. When politicians invoke God, the default image is that of a supreme being or a higher power that supports whatever power these politicians represent and the principles of their parties. Economists are less likely to talk about God, although they often utilize Adam Smith's notion of the "invisible hand of the market," which refers to a transcendent principle that guarantees the success of capitalist market transactions.

The default images of God follow the flow of dominant power. In this regard, there is little difference between conservatives and liberals. Each group may define power slightly differently, with conservatives holding to a more blatant in-your-face power that includes violence, war, and authoritarian structures in general, and liberals holding to a gentler and kinder power that often rejects violence and war and endorses softer forms of authority that stress the status quo's values. But in both cases, power and authority continue to move from the top down, from the elites to the multitude, from the educated to the uneducated, and from the wealthy to the destitute. Conservatives and liberals share little awareness that God might be different from these top-down schemes. It is for this reason that they have failed to recognize the theological challenge of the Occupy movement, although they are aware of some of the social and political challenges.

These attitudes can be seen in the various shapes that the so-called culture wars have taken. Conservative Christians, for instance, have long argued for creationism as well as for the intelligent design of the universe by a higher power. This is well known; what is less well known, however, is that these arguments are informed (mostly by default) by top-down images of God as the creator of the status quo. In other words, the God of creationism is also the God who creates the world in which conservative politics and economics flourish, and the God of intelligent design is the God who produces a quasi-Aristotelian great chain of being, according to which higher and lower forms of life and even of humanity can easily be distinguished. In the intelligent design of this chain, God is at the very top, followed by hierarchies that set in stone social differences, with men being placed above women, adults above children, the rich above the poor, clergy above laity, and people of one's own ethnicity over people of another ethnicity.

Liberal Christians, however, have long accepted Darwinian theories of evolution, noting correctly that evolution does not necessarily have to rule out the involvement of the divine in the process of creation. Creation, in this view, does not take place in seven days, as the book of Genesis metaphorically states, but happens over millions of years and is ongoing. What is often overlooked, however, is that liberal Christians' endorsements of evolution are frequently also related to top-down images of God. This is especially the case when the biological theory of evolution is conflated with the ideas of a so-called social Darwinism, according to which the wealthy and the powerful in the current system embody the rule of the survival of the fittest. In its theological form, social Darwinism is built into creation and thus endorsed by the creator. Since the default position is top-down, Darwin's theories are often linked with social Darwinism, although this is not necessarily what Darwin implied.

These images of God are not about to wither away by themselves; we can change them only if we see God involved in the midst of the struggles of life. Jürgen Moltmann's suggestion that Christ is not to be found at the peaks of evolution but at its weakest points is one way to change dominant images of God.[10] But why not reject social Darwinism altogether and rethink the concept of evolution as favoring the elites together with the concept of God as favoring the elites? Thinking theologically in the midst of the struggles of life changes everything.

New images of God emerge as Christians and many other religious people encounter God in fresh ways in the midst of the struggles of life that are brought to public attention by the Occupy movement. When we see God as engaging the lives of the 99 percent, we may become aware of the dependence of many of our God images on the 1 percent, realizing that these images have often been not much more than projections of our own wishful thinking onto the sky. Nineteenth-century critics of religion, such as Ludwig

Feuerbach, had a point: religion can easily turn into the projection of our own values onto the divine, so that God becomes our own creation. Today we realize that this is the case in particular situations when religion and dominant power are fused.

The good news is that there are other options. As theologian John Wesley realized in the eighteenth century, religion that goes "from the greatest to the least" makes things look as if "the power would appear to be of men."[11] Dominant power usually gets what it wants, and so religion is no exception. But Wesley also noted that there is an altogether different strand of religion that can be found in the biblical traditions, one that he felt had manifested itself in the Methodist movement of his time: "'They shall all know me,' saith the Lord, not from the greatest to the least (this is that wisdom of the world which is foolishness with God) but 'from the least to the greatest,' that the praise may not be of men, but of God."[12] Wesley finds support in a passage from Hebrews where God talks about how people will know him "from the least of them to the greatest" (Heb. 8:11). To be sure, this is a pretty radical statement that is as relevant in our own time as it was in Wesley's. Keep in mind, however, that Wesley did not invent this particular radicalism: he found it in the New Testament traditions and Jesus himself, who got it from the Jewish traditions of the Hebrew Bible. With the Occupy movement, this ancient wisdom is once again coming into its own.

The doctrine of creation is a case in point of images of God that move from the bottom up. Hebrew Bible scholars have observed that the biblical accounts of creation do not grow out of situations of domination—or leisure, like many speculative accounts of God and the natural world. Just the opposite: the creation stories grow out of situations of struggle and oppression. Reflections on God as creator had their beginning when the people of Israel and Judah were forced to live in exile in the Babylonian Empire. It was here that they realized that their God was wholly other: their God was different from the gods of the Babylonian Empire, who seemed to be victorious in the present age. It was in the midst of the pressures of empire that they discovered that their God, who was no stranger to struggles against oppression, was the one who created heaven and earth. This God, whose identity was determined by the liberation of the slaves in Egypt, would ultimately prevail over the gods of empire and the oppressive systems they endorsed.

Later in Christian theology, the doctrine of creation that had its beginnings in resistance against oppression was interpreted in light of another event of resistance: the incarnation of Jesus Christ. Jesus Christ as the incarnate God was unlike the gods of the Roman Empire; rather than adapting to the schemes of the empire, he put up a fight and organized alternative ways of life in community.[13] He reordered the priorities of the empire, proclaiming that with God the last will be first and the first will be last (Mark 10:31). Announcing that the reign of God was at hand, Jesus stirred up an inevitable conflict, according to which the reign of God clashed with the reign of the emperor. The reign of God was not a mere competitor with the reign of the Roman emperor but a different reign altogether, in which good news was brought to the poor, release to captives, sight to the blind, and freedom to the oppressed; the year of God's favor was pronounced, according to which expropriated property had to be returned and slaves had to be freed (Luke 4:18–19). Jesus established this reign of God firmly on the grounds of the Hebrew Bible, referencing both the prophet Isaiah (Isa. 61:1–2) and the traditions of the Jubilee Year (Lev. 25:1–55). Confronted with this clash of two different forms of power and two different ways of life, it was no wonder that those who asked a question about paying taxes were shaken up a bit by Jesus's implied claim to give to God what belonged to God—namely, everything (Mark 12:13–17; the NRSV translates it as "they were utterly amazed").

Rethinking God from the bottom up, from the incarnation of God in a carpenter day laborer at home in a provincial part of the country, is at the very heart of Christianity and guides our efforts to reimagine the divine. Let us be clear, however, that what moves from the bottom up is not just the human in Christ; it is also the divine. This is what is commonly overlooked when theologians contrast theological approaches from below and from above, where "below" designates humanity and "above" designates divinity. But if we stop playing off humanity and divinity in Jesus Christ—as both liberals and conservatives continue to do in their own ways—it is no longer possible to divide things as if the approach from the human is linked to what comes from below and the approach from the divine is linked to what comes from above. Both humanity and divinity can move from the top down, as numerous empires have clearly shown. But both humanity and divinity can also move from the bottom up. This has been shown by the Jesus movement as well as by many other resistance movements throughout history, beginning with the Hebrew slaves in Egypt, the Hebrew Bible prophets, the apostle Paul (who also sided with the people),[14] some strands of monasticism, the left wing of the Reformation, Methodism, and Pentecostalism. Although not all of the strands of these developments move from the bottom up, all these traditions have their roots in bottom-up movements. Other movements, like the abolitionist, suffragist, and civil rights movements in the United States, share a similar awareness of God and humanity moving together from the bottom up. Today, the Occupy movement can be considered the legitimate heir to all these developments, with deep implications for our contemporary understanding of God.

Rethinking God from the bottom up, from God's incarnation in a particular human being who maintained solidarity with the multitude, provides alternatives to two problematic points of view that are virtually omnipresent. The first is based on the Aristotelian great chain of being. Here, the divine is at the top, followed by a hierarchy of spiritual beings, which includes further down the hierarchy of men over women, citizens over non-citizens, and masters over slaves. Today, we see this hierarchy perhaps most clearly in the exorbitant salaries paid to CEOs and the ever-decreasing wages at the lower end of the job market, with top investors earning the top dollar. [15] If ownership were the point of comparison, the hierarchy of class would be even more apparent. Despite commonplace affirmations of gender and racial equality, this hierarchy is also persistent in the differing pay scales for men and women and for workers of different racial and ethnic backgrounds.

The second problematic point of view emphasizes organic relationship over crude hierarchy. Here, the organic relatedness of all lives is celebrated, as well as the fact that different parts contribute to the whole in their own ways. The problem with this model is that it is harks back to the Roman Empire, where the organic model of the body was useful for maintaining order—rebellious members of the body could be told that they had no option but to stay in their natural place. As we have seen, the apostle Paul turns this image on its head when he reminds the church in Corinth that "the members of the body that seem to be weaker are indispensable," that "God has so arranged the body, giving the greater honor to the inferior member," and that "if one member suffers, all suffer together with it" (1 Cor. 12:22, 12:24, 12:26).

In the midst of these struggles, the Third Commandment, which prohibits taking God's name in vain, gains new meaning ("You shall not make wrongful use of the name of the Lord your God" [Exod. 20:7]). The most disastrous way of taking God's name in vain and using it wrongfully is when the God who resists empires from beginning to end is imagined as emperor-like. Can there be any offense that could be worse than promoting images of God that are diametrically opposed to how God reveals Godself? This means, of course, that the problem may well begin with the churches and religious people themselves, who are taking God's name in vain when they create an idol that resembles more the image of the powerful than the God of Abraham, Hagar, Tamar, Amos, Jesus, Mary, and Paul. What if taking God's name in vain includes even the time-honored images of God in the great cathedrals of the world as male, emperor-like, and embodying top-down power?

GOD-IN-RELATION

Among the most important insights of modern theology is that we can know God only in relation to us.[16] We cannot know God in Godself, just as we cannot know other people in themselves or things as they are in themselves. This is, of course, how most of the authors of the Bible prefer to speak about God as well: not as God in Godself but as God-in-relation to the lives and histories of real people. The writers of the Gospels, for instance, talk about God-in-relation to people under the rule of the Roman Empire in the first century. The Psalms in the Hebrew Bible talk about how God manifests Godself in the lives of people under pressure in various historical contexts. Even the Book of Revelation, often misread as a document that deals with events in the future, talks about how God relates to people—in particular, churches in the Middle East at the time of its writing—and how God struggles with the power brokers of the Roman Empire, of whose influence the readers of the Book of Revelation would have been only too painfully aware.

The quest for justice, which is at the core of the Occupy movement, is also at the core of many religious traditions, and the parallels run deep. In Jewish traditions, the term "justice" refers to a relationship between God and humans and humans with each other, rooted in God's faithfulness to the covenant.[17] Justice is practiced in the formation of relationship and the restoration of abusive relationships not only with God but also with human beings. Today, one of the most fundamental forms that abusive relationships have taken is the split between the 99 percent and the 1 percent, which results in a small group getting wealthier and more powerful just as everyone else is forced to cut back to such an extent that growing numbers of people are losing their livelihoods and tens of thousands of people around the globe die every day from hunger and preventable causes.

In order to restore relationship in this situation, it is not enough to seek balance or a middle ground, or to admonish people to "get along." In the work of restoring relationship, God is envisioned in many traditions not merely as a mediator, taking up a safe position in the middle, but as a partisan who takes the side of those who have been abused and exploited. This God not only takes the side of the proverbial widows, the orphans, and the strangers—a recurring theme throughout the Hebrew Bible—he also takes the side of the slaves on whose shoulders the economy rests, calling for their liberation every fiftieth year (Lev. 25:10, 25:39–41).[18] Furthermore, this God takes the side of the poor, who are not poor because they are lazy but because they are exploited by the wealthy (Psalms 35:10; Prov. 22:16; Amos 4:1; James 2:5–6, 5:4). This is perhaps the most important issue in the current climate because the poor as well as the unemployed and the underemployed are increasingly being blamed for their fate. Another one of the Abrahamic traditions, Islam, also speaks of a God who takes the side of the oppressed. The Qur'an notes God's fight for the oppressed and invites the community to participate: "And what is [the matter] with you that you fight not in the cause of Allah and [for] the oppressed among men, women, and children?" (Qur'an 4:75). In all these examples, the liberation of the poor and the oppressed is not just a social concern: it is at the heart of what it is to know God and to worship God. As Ashgar Ali Engineer says about Islam, "There is no real surrender to the will of God without justice."[19]

The traditional biblical and Qur'anic notions of justice model relationships and, therefore, go beyond matters of fairness and equality. This is how far modern images of God-in-relation have usually been able to go, but many of the more radical images of God in the Bible go one step further. God's justice is about a struggle against injustice, which requires addressing the imbalance of power that leads to injustice rather than covering it up. Addressing the imbalance of power and refusing to keep covering it up is the major contribution of the Occupy movement as well. The crucial importance of this movement becomes clearer when we consider one of the key differences between the Occupy movement and more traditional proclamations of the American Dream: while the hope of the American Dream is the hope that anybody can make it up the ladder, the Occupy movement reminds us that this dream is a reality for fewer and fewer people. When relationships are so distorted that the 1 percent and their children increase their wealth and power at the expense of the 99 percent and their children, the proclamation of modern (and American) values like fairness and equality is no longer suffi-cient.

In situations of grave imbalances of power, a well-meaning effort to mediate is not enough; taking sides with those who do not benefit from the imbalance of power is the only way to change and to make things right. For this reason, God sides with the slaves in Egypt, as the stories of Exodus recall, just as Jesus regularly sides with the multitude, as the Gospels remind us. Being in relationship by taking the side of the oppressed is the mark of God's justice. Justice is the restoration of relationship so that the oppressed are not only included but also seen as essential for the well-being of the community.[20]

Liberal efforts to rid our images of God of notions of judgment, claiming the distinction between a judgmental and a benevolent God, do not help us here. A God who pronounces judgment on injustice and sides with those who experience it is the only hope for those whose lives are endangered and destroyed. Maintaining a close relationship with the oppressed does not mean, however, that God refuses to be in relationship with the oppressors and those in positions of dominant power. Yet relationships with those in positions of dominant power shape up differently: if God "has filled the hungry with good things, and sent the rich away empty" (Luke 1:53), or if Jesus blesses the poor and proclaims woe to the rich (Luke 6:20, 6:24), judgment on the rich is proclaimed for the sake of a conversion that is required if broken relationships are to be rebuilt and restored. In other words, only if the 1 percent are made aware of and begin to understand the distorted nature of their relationships can they enter into more appropriate relation-ships.

God's power is best understood in these contexts. The life and ministry of Jesus are full of examples of this alternative power. Jesus does not take on the role of the hero who single-handedly overthrows the powers that be by assuming unilateral and top-down control; rather, Jesus works in the context of a community, as an organizer. He organizes the multitude—the 99 per-cent—in such a way that they, too, become sons and daughters of God and share in God's power. The new kind of community that is organized on the basis of these relationships is fundamentally different from the patriarchal family that is organized on the basis of biological kinship, and it is funda-mentally different from the special interest groups of the 1 percent. While Jesus had the courage to challenge even his own family along these lines

(Mark 3:33–35; see also chapter 4 of this book), in some places in the Gospels he went further: "For I have come to set a man against his father, and a daughter against her mother, and a daughter-in-law against her mother-in-law; and one's foes will be members of one's own household" (Matt. 10:35–36).

Does not the Occupy movement represent these dynamics better than many of the churches? The Occupy movement does not have central, heroic leaders who call the shots, and it rejects centralized leadership as the way forward. Relationships within the Jesus movement may be loose, but the commitment to the movement—doing the will of God (Mark 3:35) is the criterion for the new community—is more significant than the typical commitments to biological families of origin or particular interest groups, which are often deeply troubled even when things appear to be well on the outside.[21] The Occupy movement's notion of the 99 percent extends this commitment even further, both to those who have already joined the community and to all those whom Jesus invites from the places of marginalization (see the parables of the lost sheep, the lost coin, and the "lost son" in Luke [15:1–32]), and particularly the ones who are "weary and are carrying heavy burdens" (Matt. 11:28).

Organizing resistance to the Roman Empire and every subsequent empire and embodying alternative ways of life is a matter of not only new relationships among human beings but also new relationships with God. These new ways of being in relationship cannot be added together with dominant relationships. In other words, relating to others and to God from the bottom up is not compatible with top-down ways of relating to others and to God. In Jesus's own words, "No one can serve two masters," and it is impossible to "serve God and wealth" (Matt. 6:24). Or, in the language of the sixteenth-century resistance movement against the Spanish Conquest, as formulated by Bartolomé de Las Casas, the gentle way of Jesus is "the only way," which cannot be combined with the dominant way of the conquistadors.[22] Today, we need to go even further than Las Casas, who sought to replace the harsh relationships of conquest with the softer relationships of a more enlightened colonialism.

No reflection on relationship is complete without the notion of class. The key issue in terms of class, as we have pointed out throughout this book, is not income level or social stratification but the matter of relationship between the classes. The Occupy movement represents this insight, but it is here that it finds the greatest pushback, manifest in never-ending accusations that this movement is about the instigation of class struggle. One can only imagine the Egyptian pharaoh at the time of the Exodus thinking along similar lines as the critics of the Occupy movement: "Before Moses and his God started to organize the Hebrew slaves, everybody got along so well. The slaves did their work, the masters supported them, and everything was fine. This Moses and his God are instigating class struggle." Or imagine King Herod's response at the time of Jesus: "Before this Jesus and his God started to organize the multitude, religion was a place of harmony and peace. Now Jesus is preaching division and the sword, instigating class struggle."

Apparently the God who seeks to restore relationships does so not by covering up the tensions that are deepening along the lines of class in favor of the status quo's religious fantasies regarding reconciliation and peace. Rather, the God who seeks to restore relationships does so by taking the side of Lazarus against the rich man and the side of the poor against Zacchaeus. The rich man and Zacchaeus—the 1 percent—are invited to join God's movement, but not in terms of business as usual. The story of Zacchaeus tells of an incredible reversal, as Zacchaeus engages not just in acts of repentance but also in those of restitution: fourfold he promises to restore what he took (Luke 19:8). Reconciliation means nothing without these acts. The story of Lazarus and the rich man remind us that the 1 percent have the option to listen to the prophets and to turn to God, but that there are limits even to what God can do in the face of the nastiest forms of class struggle; not even God can make a difference if the rich brothers of the rich man are not willing to listen (Luke 16:27–31).

In sum, when we reimagine God-in-relation, we need to recall the directionality of the relationship. The Psalms pick up this directionality, with a theme that has been part of the dangerous memory of alternative religious communities for centuries: "Out of the depths I cry to you, O Lord" (130:1). There is hope for those who approach God from the underside of history—and so there may be hope even for the 1 percent when they get off their high horses and begin to understand their own need for transformation. "There is forgiveness with [God]," the psalmist continues (130:4), speaking for those who approach God *de profundis* (out of the depths of the struggle) and there is ultimately redemption (130:8), yet not the cheap kind.

GOD AND THE MULTITUDE

In situations where images of God have been used to justify the status quo, theologians have often pointed out the otherness of God. One of the most prominent theologians to argue this point was Karl Barth, whose contributions were discussed in chapter 4. More recently, queer theologians like the late Marcella Althaus-Reid, who taught in Scotland, have helped us understand the queerness of God—an image that still comes as a shock even to many open-minded people. Her notion of the otherness of God is tied to what she calls God's indecency, noting that "God becomes chaos" rather than the order of the dominant system. The task of theologians is, therefore, the "indecenting of the production of God and Jesus."[23] Regardless of whether one is in full agreement with Althaus-Reid's often rather challenging images, she is right in that the "decent" God has been put to use by the powers that be for too long. Mayra Rivera, a Latina theologian in the United States, has picked up the theme of the otherness of God in a slightly different way, using the insights of postcolonial theory. She notes that God's otherness is tied to experiences of human otherness. As a result, God is somehow found in "the presence of the untouchables," linking us to other people and embracing not their sameness but their otherness.[24] For both Althaus-Reid and Rivera, the otherness of God is not a matter of otherworldliness but of a divinity that is different from the images of the status quo and that makes a difference in the lives of the people.

Throughout history, religion has often made it too easy for the ruling classes to claim God for their own purposes. Their success, their wealth, and their power seemed to be proof enough that God was on their side. Even some of the Founding Fathers of the United States shared this view. In the words of Benjamin Franklin, "I have lived, Sir, a long time, and the longer I live, the more convincing proofs I see of this truth—that God governs in the affairs of men. And if a sparrow cannot fall to the Ground without his Notice, is it probable that an Empire can rise without his Aid?"[25] This trajectory continues in a fairly straight line all the way to the present. During his time in office, former vice president Dick Cheney once sent out Christmas cards quoting Franklin's statement and thus claiming God's support for the policies of the administration of President George W. Bush.[26] While empires' display of power is impressive, we must not forget that these kinds of dominant power invariably have come to an end. The Holy Roman Empire is no more, and even the once well-honed structures of European colonialism have largely disappeared. Current power politics, many of them based in the United States, have not fared too well either, as the Great Recession demonstrates.

Of course, as dominant histories have failed, there are no alternative histories that can claim easy success and triumph either. But movements that have embodied power from below—reclaiming alternative perspectives on how God's own power operates—have made more significant and lasting contributions that are too often overlooked. The women's movement, for instance, has managed to strengthen the position of women in many different ways, from acquiring voting rights for women and integrating women more fully into democratic political processes to promoting cultural changes that have boosted the agency of women in matters of everyday life and even in matters of religion. Many religious traditions now ordain women and allow women to exercise religious leadership. To be sure, the women's movement has taken very different and sometimes contradictory shapes in different places. Many Muslim women, for instance, have maintained the importance of the veil in their struggle of resistance—a position that Western feminists have often found difficult to accept.[27] Nevertheless, a common thrust in terms of the question of the emancipation of women remains part of women's movements everywhere. Many other examples of movements could be given, reminding us that the alternative power that we find at work in the divine is not just a pious idea or wishful thinking but also quite real and long-lasting in history.

Perhaps the most important argument for the significance of the contributions of all of these movements, including the Occupy movement, is that it is impossible to restore an appreciation for the otherness of God without restoring at the same time an appreciation for the otherness of other people. Theological affirmations of the otherness of God have often backfired because people had no idea what it meant to appreciate and respect otherness in people.

To give another example, liberals who express a sincere desire to help others often do so in ways that fail to take other people seriously. As a result, they impose their own ideas on others, trying to provide for them as they see fit. Worse yet, liberals often try to help others by shaping them in their own image. We can observe these dynamics in more than specific social projects, such as Head Start programs and various mission projects of the churches; these dynamics are particularly pronounced in the structures of a more enlightened colonialism and in postcolonial efforts at development. Even the language of development contains this lack of appreciation for others: one group that considers itself more developed, usually from the Global North, comes to the aid of another group that is considered less developed, usually located in the Global South.[28]

Conservatives, on the other hand, may be sincere in pronouncing a high view of God, but this view is rarely tied to high views of other people, which is why it fails. The sort of American exceptionalism that is often adhered to by conservatives holds that Americans, especially the 1 percent that represents the so-called American Dream, are privileged by God, while others do not seem to enjoy such privileges. Many of the Barthians who followed Barth's appreciation for the otherness of God fell into similar traps and lost their critical edge because they overlooked the fact that Barth's appreciation for the otherness of God was linked to an appreciation of the otherness of working-class people.[29] And while these Barthians may not be in agreement with conservative positions that uphold the superiority of people in their own camp, this is the result of any position that is unable to open up to other people.

While the culture wars are stuck in this impasse, only the development of a new appreciation for others can help us find a new appreciation for God. According to 1 John 4:20, "Those who say, 'I love God,' and hate their brothers or sisters, are liars; for those who do not love a brother or sister whom they have seen, cannot love God whom they have not seen." Put in terms of appreciation and respect rather than the overused notion of love, this means that it is not possible to appreciate and respect God without appreciating and respecting other people. To be sure, the sort of appreciation and respect that counts is not a romantic feeling toward others or a laissez-faire attitude of tolerance that prevents others from challenging us; appreciation and respect imply that others can lay a claim on us, partly because we are not individuals, as the 1 percent believe, but rather inextricably connected in a community that we are calling the multitude. In the wake of the Occupy movement, the 99 percent are becoming clearer about this idea.

This connection between respecting God as other and other people points to an inextricable connection between piety and justice, which is deeply rooted in the Abrahamic traditions. In the Jewish tradition of Amos, the voice of God proclaims, "I hate, I despise your festivals, and I take no delight in your solemn assemblies. . . . But let justice roll down like waters, and righteousness like an everflowing stream" (5:21 and 5:24). In the days of the civil rights movement, the Rev. Martin Luther King Jr. never tired of quoting these passages. In the Muslim tradition, the Qur'an reads, "O ye who believe! stand out firmly for God, as witnesses to fair dealing, and let not the hatred of others to you make you swerve to wrong and depart from justice. Be just: that is next to piety: and fear God. For God is well-acquainted with all that ye do" (5:8).[30] Justice and piety belong together in many religious traditions.

This combination of justice and piety, together with the development of a new appreciation and respect for others, is embodied in fresh ways in the Occupy movement. The Occupy movement is a place where people can become aware of more than simply their connectedness to other members of the 99 percent; here, people are also challenged to acknowledge the differences, without which no true relationship can survive. This is what is at the heart of deep solidarity. Working side-by-side with people of other ethnicities, sexualities, and genders is not possible unless people develop a deep sense of appreciation and respect for difference; since this is not taught much in our schools or religious communities, people are learning as they go. The nonchalant attitudes of tolerance that liberal communities often display toward lesbian, gay, bisexual, and transgender people, for instance, are preferable to homophobia and rejection, but do not count toward this deep appreciation of otherness. In addition, the Occupy movement has also helped the 99 percent develop an initial understanding of their difference from, as well as connection to, the 1 percent. This realization may well be one of the most crucial insights when it comes to our images of God because it is commonly kept under wraps in American society. Theology of the multitude reminds us that God is not an impartial judge, staying out of the conflicts of this world, but an active participant in the struggle for justice.

As a result of this newly emerging appreciation and respect for others—this is one of the important characteristics that set apart the multitude from the masses, the rabble, or the mob—new attitudes develop that eventually result in new relations to the divine. The person who learns that others are neither objects for exploitation nor objects for development or service projects may open up enough to be able to accept challenges from the other. These challenges are very different from the challenges that come from the top, to which we are all more or less attuned because we have no choice, like the challenges imposed on us by bosses, bishops, and presidents. And the challenges imposed by a top-down God take similar forms. Is this not one of the key reasons why many people keep going to church simply because they feel they have little choice if they want to avoid eternal damnation?

The challenges that come to us from others, however, are different. They are the sort of challenges that we can still choose to avoid by pretending that they are invisible, by playing them down as trivial or insignificant, or by disqualifying them as strange and outlandish. The challenges of a bottom-up God resemble these sorts of challenges, and so it is not surprising that Christianity sought to avoid them as soon as it came into positions of power—for instance, by making invisible the life and ministry of Jesus: neither the Apostles' Creed nor the Nicene Creed (the creeds that many believe are at the core of the Christian faith) even reference it. The challenges of a bottom-up God are easily played down as trivial or insignificant—the famous passage about the last judgment in Matthew (25:31–46) has never received the lion's share of the churches' attention, although, like much church talk, it also talks about who is "in" and who is "out." Finally, the challenges of a bottom-up God have often been disqualified as strange and outlandish: many traditions have simply declared Jesus's Sermon on the Mount to be impossible or fit only for a higher order of Christians, like monks, priests, and other highly committed people. Reimagining the divine in the context of the Occupy movement leads us back to these old challenges.

When we talk about God-in-relation, what would it mean to rethink notions of solidarity at the level of divinity itself? In traditional theological terminology, this is the place of the doctrine of the Trinity. This doctrine, although it received its official formulation under the leadership of Emperor Constantine at the Council of Nicaea in 325 CE, might help us in our efforts to reimagine the divine. When read against the grain, the early church's confession in the Nicene Creed that Jesus is fully divine and of the same substance as the Father (*homoousios to patri*) opened the door to rethinking the first person of the Trinity, traditionally called the Father. God, when seen in the light of the life and ministry of Jesus, can no longer be conceived as a heavenly monarch who rules from the top down. This God no longer served as support of the monarchy of the Roman emperor, which may be the reason why Constantine at the end of his life gave up on the doctrine of the Trinity and reverted back to Arianism.[31] By the same token, if Jesus challenged not only empire but also the family and patriarchy, God can no longer be conceived as a heavenly patriarch; if anything, envisioning God as "father" does not endorse patriarchy but challenges all patriarchal notions of fatherhood. Rather than feeling reaffirmed, rulers and fathers should be shaken to the bone when these terms are used for God.

The cross of Jesus raises some deep questions for our understanding of God, as theologian Jürgen Moltmann pointed out four decades ago.[32] Not only does Jesus's suffering affect the Godhead—otherwise, it would make little sense to speak of the unity of the Trinity and its being of the same substance—but the first person of the Trinity also does not come to the rescue of Jesus on the cross, although Jesus seems to have expected this as a possibility (Mark 14:36). The fact that God does not prevent the crucifixion means either that God does not want to save Jesus (perhaps because God has a "plan" that involves sacrificing Jesus) or that God for some reason does not act in the sort of top-down ways that are commonly thought of as divine action.

The first option comes dangerously close to assuming that it is ultimately God who needs Jesus dead, and thus it is God who kills Jesus, or that killing Jesus is a priestly act that is somehow justified by God. The second option is more interesting, considering that the first option paints God in a negative image and devalues the life and ministry of Jesus, and that in the Bible understanding the cross as sacrifice is just one option among many others: What if God does not act in ways that are commonly thought of as divine (i.e., like a monarch, in unilateral fashion from the top down)? In this case, Godself undergoes the struggles of suffering and death on the cross—the nails of the Son going through the hands of the Father in the back, as an ancient tradition has it.[33] The idea that God is not characterized by top-down action is thus one of the most consistent insights of a theology of the multitude. While there is some sense of this to various degrees in various liberation theologies, we are pushing further along these lines.

Nevertheless, the cross is not all about suffering and death at the hands of the Roman Empire and its allies in the Jewish religious hierarchy. The cross is an important step toward the overcoming of empire and oppression, pointing toward the resurrection, which might be understood as an uprising of Jesus against the powers that cause the suffering and death of the people. Yet this uprising is not a triumphalist one, as it moves through suffering and death. Here, everything changes. Although we cannot give up the idea of God acting in history if we want to maintain the reality of God, we need to re-envision it from the ground up. What if God is at work in history, but not from positions of control? Siding with the oppressed, with those who are unjustly persecuted by the system, and with the poor (Luke 6), God's work in history is more complex and more open-ended than we could ever imagine. History itself is open-ended for this reason, and there are no easy happy endings, like the kind that Hollywood has produced for us for decades. We become part of this history not by acquiring positions of control but by siding with the multitude, rebuilding relationships from there in the context of resistance movements.

THE OCCUPY CHALLENGE TO GOD

God will not be found, it seems to us, where God can be controlled. Those who take up their place among the 99 percent know one thing—namely, that they are not in control. They are not the masters in their own house, and their goal is not to become masters like the 1 percent. The democracy for which the Occupy movement stands is and remains the opposite of politics as top-down control: this democracy depends on broad-based participation from below, world without end. As we have seen in this chapter, Godself rejects top-down power and control and joins the people. This insight is reflected in the Letter of James, which states that "the rich will disappear like a flower in the field" (1:10). Viewed from this perspective, history looks different: sooner or later, all systems of control crumble and fail, no matter how much each of them assures its followers that God is on its side. The Holy Roman Empire is no more, and neither are the Norman or the Spanish empires, although they all identified themselves with the presence of God on earth. Northern European colonialism has ended, and the humanity that attempted to replace God in the Enlightenment faltered with it. Not even our contemporary empire of neoliberal capitalism—trying to reassure itself of the control of the invisible hand of the market—is faring particularly well because the foundations on which it rests are crumbling and the invisible hand works for Wall Street but not for Main Street. In all these cases, the changing of the guards has led to a changing of the gods.

While religion that supports the status quo is bound to fail eventually, religion that is caught in the middle does not help much either. A report quotes the president of a liberal theological seminary calling for reconciliation: "There's so much polarization in our country now, and demonization of one side of the other. . . . As religious leaders, we want to be 'repairers of the breach' [paraphrasing a passage in Isaiah]. . . . So the question is how we can come together, Wall Street and Main Street, to come up with solutions that are going to work for all of us."[34] This statement assumes that there is a place in the middle, and that God is somehow there as well. But this place is an illusion, and Jesus's reminder that no one can serve two masters needs to be heard once again, loud and clear. Religious leaders, although they usually do not like to admit this even to themselves, are rarely part of the 1 percent, but they can end up working for the 1 percent if they preach an easy reconciliation that does not take the powers that be to task. Wall Street and Main Street cannot work together as long as Wall Street calls the shots and plays the role of a god who is an idol of control and self-centeredness. If Main Street and Church Street compromise too quickly and thus let Wall Street continue with business as usual, not only will they not reach their goals, but they will also betray the real God who works in ways that will always remain mysterious and beyond reason to the powers that be.

In the context of discussing the Occupy movement, another prominent woman theologian, Katharine Jefferts-Schori, the presiding bishop of the Episcopal Church of the United States, has noted that the wealthy have a particular interest in otherworldly theology.[35] This is another well-established mechanism of dominant theology, as it preserves the status quo. Just as the participants in the Occupy movement are frequently confronted with the hostile instruction to get a real job, theologians who reflect God's involvement with movements of liberation are frequently confronted with the hostile instruction to do real theology. We have heard this many times.

What we have found, inspired by the Occupy movement, is that God is indeed different from the schemes of power that dominate the world today. Yet this does not mean that God is otherworldly; just the opposite is the case. God stands for alternative forms of power, for a kingdom that is not of "this world" (John 18:36), as this world is at the moment, but rather of a world that is already beginning and that is scaring the powers that be to death. Thanks be to God.

Chapter Six

Envisioning the Church of the Multitude

> Christian life in the basic communities is characterized by the absence of alienating structures, by direct relationships, by reciprocity, by a deep communion, by mutual assistance, by communality of gospel ideals, by equality among its members.
>
> —Leonardo Boff, *Ecclesiogenesis*[1]

The Rev. Edmund Harris went to support Occupy Providence in Rhode Island when the campsite was established on its opening day with about two thousand people. Harris had visited South Africa when he was in college and was impressed by the involvement of the churches and grassroots communities in the anti-apartheid movement. It was important for him to come out in solidarity with a movement that stood up for the marginalized in society. With the Rev. Jennifer Pedrick, he organized the Eucharist in the campsite for people who wanted to receive it. The experience broadened his horizons; he saw what a church without walls might look like. The people came from many different walks of life, and some were homeless, without a long-term place to stay. They were from different generations, both young and old. The people in the church without walls had the kind of diversity seldom seen in middle-class congregations.[2]

Just as other social movements before it have done, the Occupy movement provides much food for thought and pushes for a new and expansive understanding of the church. The anti-slavery movement and the civil rights movement in the United States radically denounced the hypocrisy of the white churches. The Rev. Martin Luther King Jr. famously said, "It is appalling that the most segregated hour of Christian America is eleven o'clock on Sunday morning." This is still true even today. The black church has often been a spiritual and transformative community for black people's struggle for freedom. In Latin America, base Christian communities have emerged as a movement from the bottom up, in opposition to the rigid structures of the hierarchical church. The feminist movement has inspired a women-church movement, in response to church traditions that deny women opportunities for leadership and ministry. The development of new church models and ecclesial forms points to the crisis and inadequacy of current models and the need to develop something new that may ultimately be more faithful to the roots of our traditions.

Likewise, our reimagining of theology and God of the multitude pushes us to envision a church or ecclesial community *for* and *by* the multitude, one that does not align with the interests of the 1 percent by default. Some of the questions we need to consider include the following: What is the nature of the church and how is the theology of the multitude socially embodied? How would members of this ecclesial community relate to each other and to the wider world? What kind of ecclesial practices and rituals will mark this community? While we want to suggest some ways to think about these questions, we need to emphasize that we have no blueprints or definitive answers to these questions, and we do not intend to create a super-mega-church for the multitude. The concrete ecclesial embodiment of the church of the multitude must be contextual in nature, rooted in the local, and open to the insights of the global struggle against the exploitation of the 1 percent.

THE CHURCH AND CLASS

We will begin with a review of the meaning of the term "church" and discuss how the church today has taken its current ecclesial form, in order to prepare the way to envision a new paradigm. The word "church" originates from the Greek term *ekklesia*, which means "assembly." The etymology of the term suggests, according to Peter C. Hodgson, "a summons or calling-out for the purpose of a gathering, especially a political assembly."[3] In Palestinian Judaism, he points out, the term "synagogue" was used to designate the place of worship in the Jewish religion, with its distinctly cultic overtones. In Hellenistic Judaism, the term *ekklesia* was used to "designate assemblies of both political and cultic character."[4] In the context of the Jewish Diaspora, these assemblies enabled the Jewish people to praise God and express their religious identity and to decide and regulate the affairs of the community. The early Christian movement used the term *ekklesia* rather than "synagogue" to describe the new community because it included both Jewish members and Gentiles, and some of the Jewish customs (such as circumcision) were eliminated as requirements for membership in this new and diverse community. The new communities were called churches of God (*ecclesiae* of God) in Jesus Christ (1 Thess. 2:14). It is important to remember that the term *ecclesia* has both religious and political meanings.

The early church movement consisted of small groups of followers of Jesus forming alternative communities to live out social visions different from those prescribed by the Roman Empire. The Acts of the Apostles states that the members of the Jerusalem church "were of one heart and one soul, and no one claimed private ownership of any possessions, but everything they owned was held in common" (4:32). Those who had possessions sold their lands and properties and shared their resources with the community, so there was "not a needy person among them" (4:34). But such high ideals quickly encountered problems when couples like Ananias and Sapphira were not willing to share what they had and kept some of the proceeds for a piece of property sold. This incident shows that the egalitarian and mutually caring ideals of the early Christian movement were undermined when the propertied class kept following its logic, striving for the preservation of private property at all costs.

In the Corinthian church, class division was a significant factor, as seen, for instance, in the controversy over whether Christians could eat food that had been offered to other gods (1 Cor. 8:1–11, 10:25–32). The Corinthian church consisted of converts from diverse groups, with the privileged upper class dominating over the lower classes. Gerd Theissen notes that "the lower classes seldom ate meat in their everyday lives," while "the members of the higher classes would have had ample opportunity for meat consumption."[5] Christians of the lower classes (the "weak") could not afford meat, and they might only have meat on those occasions when meat was freely distributed at pagan religious festivals. For the weak, meat was therefore associated with pagan worship, and eating it would be religiously dangerous, while for the upper classes (the "strong"), meat was of no concern. Though Theissen was criticized for focusing too much on idol meat while idol food consisted of other foods,[6] his reference to class analysis in looking at what were often considered exclusively religious issues is enlightening.

Class was also a factor in determining the roles women played in the early Christian communities and women's relations with one another. Women served as missionaries and leaders of house churches in the early church.[7] Several prominent converts were women (Acts 17:4, 17:12). Wealthy women and women of high standing founded, sustained, and supported the house churches, which sometimes served as missionary centers. For example, one of the most prominent missionaries and founders of house churches was Prisca, who with her companion Aquila supported Paul's work (Rom. 16:3). The religious roles of poorer women are less well known because of the scarcity of historical records and androcentric biases. Class was an issue that divided women in the early church. Latin American theologian Elsa Tamez notes that some rich women, as owners of households, would demand "submission of their children, slaves, and persons who had received favors from them."[8] The author of 1 Timothy had these rich women in mind when he cautioned that "women should dress themselves modestly and decently in suitable clothing, not with their hair braided, or with gold, pearls, or expensive clothes" (2:9). Their elaborate hairdos, fashion, and jewelry distinguished the rich women from poor, ordinary women. The author of 1 Timothy saw the presence of these rich women as threatening since they probably tried to use their wealth and status to dominate other members of the community. But instead of addressing the relatively small number of women benefactors or patrons, the author turned to the patriarchal ideology of his time to subjugate all women to men, regardless of their social class.[9] "Let women learn in silence with full submission. I permit no woman to teach or have authority over a man; she is to keep silent" (1 Tim. 2:11–12).

The patriarchal attitudes that subjugated women in the families were extended to the ecclesia of God. As the church became institutionalized in the second century, women's leadership was relegated to marginal positions and restricted to the traditional spheres of women, with the patriarchalization of local church and leadership.[10] Authority and influence increasingly resided in the bishops and local church officials. The line between the clergy and laity was clearly drawn, as if they belonged to two separate classes within the Christian community. As Christianity became the religion of the Roman Empire, the life and structure of the church were influenced by the social reality of Christendom. Lewis S. Mudge notes that the Catholic Church polity evolved based on "an organic notion of society in which direction and integrity are guaranteed by the symbolic head, monarch, archbishop, Pope."[11] The organized church and the Roman Empire interacted closely based on the shared "Christian" values of Christendom.

Over time, the Roman Catholic Church developed into a highly coordinated, hierarchical structure with different divisions, each with their managerial structures. From the Middle Ages on, the church became immensely wealthy and a huge landholder. Robert B. Ekelund Jr., Robert F. Hébert, and Robert D. Tollison have studied the economics of religion, and they compare the medieval church to a vast corporation:

> The pope is the CEO, the curia and cardinals are upstream directors of various functions including a financial division collecting revenues called the papal camera (treasury), and a geographically dispersed downstream retail division, local bishops, parish priests, and monks of various orders "sell" products and services.[12]

It was against such a bureaucratic setup that the Reformation of the sixteenth century emerged, calling for the establishment of a new church. If the medieval church polity was more suitable for semi-feudal and rent-seeking societies, its form became outdated when Europe transitioned into early capitalism. One immediate cause of the Reformation was Luther's attack on the selling of indulgences. The selling of indulgences was not only a religious abuse, but it also represented a sophisticated system of extracting money from the people, although there were separate scales for the wealthy, who paid the highest price, while the middle class paid less, and the poor were charged the least of all.[13] People were forced to pay for the indulgences and rents to the church because salvation could only come through the church.

In preaching justification by faith, the reformers emphasized the relation between an individual and God, and eliminated the church as the go-between. Salvation was by faith and through God's grace, limiting the role of the church and sacraments. Luther also insisted on the priesthood of all believers instead of a rigid boundary separating the clergy and the laity, resulting in the democratization of church organization to some extent. Instead of the traditional seven sacraments, the reformers reduced that number to two—baptism and the Eucharist—and therefore eliminated costly ceremonies and practices. This new ecclesial form was welcome news for the wealthy and property-holding class, because they would have more money to spend and be less controlled by the church. Many of the German nobles responded favorably to

Luther's appeal to support him in his fight against the Roman Catholic Church. To a large degree, the Lutheran Church of the Reformation spread due to these connections and not from the bottom up.[14]

In his book *The Protestant Ethic and the Spirit of Capitalism*, Max Weber notes another connection of religion and class when he argues that because Calvinist ethics support hard work, saving, and vocation in secular life, capital accumulation and economic growth occurred faster in Protestant regions than Catholic areas in Western Europe.[15] There is a sense in which the Protestant understanding of church was more attractive to the emerging bourgeoisie because the Reformation "freed up resources such as saving, capital, and labor supply that could be directed to productive uses."[16] Most of the mainline Protestant denominations in North America and Europe, therefore, largely inherit a church model developed with close ties to the rise of the bourgeoisie—that is, the capitalist ruling class. Although liturgies, church organization, and communal life have changed over time, the cultural ethos and outlook of the church are to a large extent shaped by that of the emerging capitalist class, which shapes the aspirations of the middle class as well. People are expected to dress up on Sunday in business suits and dresses and to pay church dues. While churches may pray for the poor, run soup kitchens, gather alms and charity for those in need, and even support programs that improve people's living conditions, many Christians are reluctant to question the systems that have kept people poor. In addition, churches are increasingly run like corporations, and many megachurches have executive pastors who function as CEOs.

The base Christian communities in Latin America challenge the complacency of the church. These communities present a new church paradigm because they build the church from below and not from the top down. Brazilian theologian Leonardo Boff uses the term "ecclesiogenesis" to describe this new experience of being a church. The church does not exist for itself; the church consists of the poor, who want to take action to change their communities. The church is seen as sacrament in history, for it announces and anticipates the universal salvation of all people. The church takes communitarian forms because members are considered equal, each with different gifts to contribute to the community. Boff writes, "Christ's power (*exousia*) resides not only in certain members, but in the totality of the People of God as vehicle of Christ's triple ministries of witness, oneness, and worship. This power of Christ's is diversified in accordance with specific functions, but it leaves no one out."[17] This new understanding enlivens the church and empowers church members to rediscover the liberating potential of the gospel message. Gustavo Gutiérrez calls for an "uncentering" of the church, such that it does not see itself as monopolizing salvation, but rather orients itself toward service to the people. [18] The model of the base Christian communities, with their egalitarian, participatory, and communal structures, has a lot in common with what we have observed in the Occupy movement. We want to pick up these threads and discuss several dimensions of the church of the multitude.

ECCLESIA OF THE MULTITUDE

The church of the multitude needs to recapture both the religious and political meanings of the term "ecclesia." The people of God assemble not just for Sunday morning worship services, but also to discuss common affairs of the community and to take faithful action for justice. Many of the prophetic traditions of the Hebrew Bible hold that working for justice is worship. The church is the community or matrix in which the multitude is being formed and nurtured. It is where the gospel that God stands in solidarity with the 99 percent and that Jesus is a part of the *minjung* is proclaimed. It reverses the cultural logic of the 1 percent and celebrates the agency and productivity of the 99 percent through songs, rituals, symbolic actions, and the sacraments. The church of the multitude is a gathering of diverse people, and it orients them toward service in the world, particularly toward the least among us.

In chapter 4, we challenged the dichotomy constructed between transcendence and immanence; we must also challenge the rigid separation between the sacred and the secular (or the profane). This has very significant implications for the understanding of sacred space and time. Traditionally, sacred space is often associated with houses of worship—synagogues, churches, temples, or mosques. For the church of the multitude, sacred space is not bound by a place or dwelling, and sacred time is not hovering above, or transcending, historical time. Jesus liberated the monopoly of sacred space in his theological conversation with the Samaritan woman at the well. He told the woman, "The hour has come when you will worship the Father neither on this mountain or in Jerusalem. . . . But the hour is coming, and is now here, when the true worshippers will worship the Father in spirit and truth" (John 4:21–23). Jesus traveled a great deal, especially during his last three years of ministry in the region of Galilee. He not only taught in synagogues and inside houses but also preached, taught, and performed miracles in open fields, near the sea of Galilee, on the outskirts of cities, in gardens, and along the road to Emmaus.

Therefore, instead of conceiving of the church as bound by the physical space of a church building, we should think of the church as beyond walls. Just as the Occupy movement claimed the power to redefine space and create new cultural forms, the church of the multitude should also imagine creatively and not be bound by rigid traditions. Michael Hardt and Antonio Negri remind us, "The movements of the multitude designate new spaces, and its journey establishes new residences."[19] In the Occupy movement, the Jewish Kol Nidre service took place in open air, instead of in a synagogue. Jews, Christians, Muslims, Buddhists, and pagans shared the use of space in the faith and spirituality tents. The image of the "tent" reminds us of the moving tabernacle in which God dwelled among the people of Israel, instead of stone buildings with high steeples and stained-glass windows. Occupy Faith uses all the spaces the groups can find, meeting in church halls, university lecture rooms, seminaries, and open park spaces. The protesters have also occupied churches, in the sense that they were housed by churches after they were evicted from various campsites. Park Hope United Methodist Church in New York housed about thirty people at the church after the protesters were ejected from Zuccotti Park. Herb Miller, the pastor of the church, said, "You have this sacred space cordoned off, but it's also made sacred by the people."[20]

If we have broken down the confines of "brick-and-mortar" sacred space, we should also refrain from establishing hard and fast lines between physical and virtual spaces. With new digital and Internet technologies, we can connect with one another and build relationships that were not possible before. BK Hipsher describes this new situation: "Now we live in a world where it is possible to experience remote location relationship at a level never before understood in a faith community context. Now we can participate in church from our living rooms either via a webcast service or even as an avatar attending church in the virtual world Second Life."[21] The virtual environment makes the demarcation of "sacred" and "profane" increasingly complicated. A helpful way is to see virtual reality as multiple worlds,[22] creating possibilities for people to share information, relate to one another, and build online communities in numerous ways. The church may leave a whole new generation out if it does not harness powerful modern forms of communication and visual art forms. Rachel Wagner, author of the provocative book

Godwired, studies the relation between religion and virtual reality. For her, "what makes something 'sacred' is more a matter of intention and perspective than anything else."[23] She urges us to take seriously the intention of people who find it important to create sacred space in their own ways, virtually: "For some online religious folk, the construction of sacred space itself can be viewed as an act of transforming the 'chaos' of cyberspace into the 'cosmos' of religious order."[24] Some people may still prefer to see physical bodies gather for worship and for action, but churches increasingly use the Internet and electronic devices to connect with people, to form online communities, and to engage the world.[25]

The democraticization of physical and virtual sacred space redirects our attention from church as building to church as assembly of people of God. Instead of "going" to church, we will focus on "doing" church or "forming" church and building relationships. Instead of fencing off Christians from the world, as if they alone are the "holy" people, the church of the multitude is firmly in the world, transforming it to usher in the reign of God. As Dietrich Bonhoeffer famously said in *Letters and Papers from Prison*, "It is only by living completely in this world that one learns to have faith. . . . In so doing, we throw ourselves completely into the arms of God, taking seriously, not our own sufferings, but those of God in the world."[26] When churches pay more attention to maintenance instead of mission, and when they turn inward and function more like middle-class clubs, the presence of the divine is not felt even in what is supposed to be "sacred space." In contrast, many people whom we interviewed spoke of feeling a profound sense of God's presence when they participated in the Occupy movement in open space, in the public square. Matthew Arlyck, for example, experienced the immanent presence of God when he was in Zuccotti Park providing pastoral care and talking to the people. He said, "I experienced communal power as God being present, the sense of God as all around—within us and all around us."[27]

If sacred space needs to be reconfigured, sacred time also needs to be infused with new meanings. Traditionally, Christians have often thought that sacred time refers to Sunday worship, which is set apart from ordinary time. Moreover, salvation history is seen as separate from secular history, such that Christians are told to be concerned about spiritual things and not to bother too much with the temporal order. But Jesus subverted this understanding of sacred time when he said, "The sabbath was made for humankind, and not humankind for the sabbath" (Mark 2:27). Challenging the Pharisees and their dominant understanding of religion, he cured the man with a withered hand on Sabbath day instead of observing the Sabbath rules (Mark 3:1–6).

Jesus was incarnated in human history at a particular time, and thus he blurred the line between "salvation" history and "secular" history. "The Word became flesh and lived among us" (John 1:14). Jesus was incarnated as a human being and immersed himself in the transformative politics of his time. Instead of understanding time in a chronological sense, Jesus called our attention to what Paul Tillich has called *kairos*: a "manifestation of the Kingdom of God."[28] There was urgency in Jesus's message about the kingdom ("The hour has come"), and the hour is always coming, and the church of the multitude needs to collectively discern the signs of our time. We have suggested that we are living in a time of life-and-death struggles, which involve both humanity and the natural environment, and we have to get involved before it is too late.

With the democraticization of sacred space and time, the old hierarchical models of the church seem outdated. Since the church of the multitude values the agency and self-organizing power of the people, there is no ecclesial structure that will fit all, for this will have to evolve through people working together. We want to offer two images—one from theology and one from social organizational theory—of what this church might look like and how it might function. Theologian Letty Russell has suggested the image of "the church in the round."[29] For her, the church is the gathering of the marginalized people around a round table to share an open and inclusive hospitality. The ecclesial community engages in action and reflection in a spiral process that brings new meanings and responses to the biblical and theological tradition. The community is formed according to "its members' configuration of what is authoritative or life-giving in that particular community and in light of their particular struggle."[30] Instead of a top-down model of leadership, Russell suggests leadership in the round, so that people can bring their different gifts and talents to serve the community. She challenges clericalism and the notion of ordination that places people in a separate order, instead focusing on the ministry of all the baptized and emphasizing relationality in all forms of ministry. Members can take on different roles and functions and can rotate them so that power does not reside in one person. Finally, she imagines the church as a "communion of hospitality," which is inclusive and open to all for people who want to participate in the struggle, regardless of race, class, gender, and sexual orientation. Our deepening awareness of class adds another challenge here, as we cannot endorse celebration of the diversity of classes when one class exploits the others, but we agree that the reality of class needs to be included in envisioning a communion of hospitality.

As Karen K. Wood says, Russell has offered a "very horizontal view of the church in its relationship to society, past ecclesial tradition, and the divine."[31] Such a horizontal view is very much in line with what we observe in the Occupy movement, in which no leaders dominate the whole group and all are welcome to contribute. Russell's model is important for a theology of the multitude because it pushes beyond more general ideas of democratization and sharpens them by attending to power differentials and the role of the margins. At a time of great power differentials, of which the Occupy movement reminds us, democracy needs to be rebuilt from below.

The other image is that of the starfish, which, although it does not come from a theological context, has much to offer in our thinking about self-organizing. Starfish have the amazing ability: most of them, if an arm is cut off, can grow a new arm. The animals can replicate themselves from even one piece of an arm because starfish are *neural decentralized networks*. Ori Brafman and Rod A. Beckstrom write, "For the starfish to move, one of the arms must convince the other arms that it's a good idea to do so. . . . The brain doesn't 'yea' or 'nay.' The starfish doesn't have a brain. There is no central command."[32] Many of us are more familiar with organizational structures that have a head and a brain, which commands the whole. In decentralized organizations, there is no one to give out orders and no clear and fixed division of roles; as a result, power is spread throughout, and all members are equal. In such an open system, communication occurs directly between members.[33] Starfish-like organizations do not need a CEO; they need a catalyst, who is usually an inspirational figure who spurs others into action. But once the groups are formed, the catalyst lets go and allows the group to manage its own affairs. Examples of starfish organizations include Native American tribes like the Apaches, music-sharing sites such as Napster, and Wikipedia. The Occupy movement is very much like a starfish organization that promotes equal access and rich connections, and is self-organizing. Such a decentralized organizational pattern has changed businesses and the world, and has tremendous potential for alternative ways of life. We venture to say that the early church movement functioned more like the starfish, with the apostles and Paul being the catalysts who visited the different small groups from time to time. Each of the groups had a different communal life and structures. The group at Corinth was quite different from the groups meeting in Jerusalem or in Ephesus, and all had different concerns and problems, while they all shared in the liberative mission of Christ. It was only later that a top-down hierarchy was put in place when the church was on its way to being institutionalized.

The need for new models of the church and new ways of organizing has been keenly felt for some time. The emergent church, for example, has attracted a number of people in England, Australia, and North America. The leaders, such as Brian McLaren and Phyllis Tickle, have argued that the time is ripe for a new form of church to meet the challenges of the postmodern world.[34] The emergent church is not so much defined by denominational identity; power and authority are more shared, and people gather in different places, combining worship, action, and community to transform the modern world according to the message of Jesus Christ. While there are many good things that have come from the emergent church and many young people are attracted to it, we find that the emergent church in North America lacks a focus on issues of class and fails to see postmodernism as the cultural logic of late capitalism, as Fredric Jameson reminds us.[35] As a result, the emergent church has appealed primarily to white Christians who are not satisfied with church life. Soong-chan Rah, who has participated in and studied the emergent church movement, notes that the leaders of the movement are largely white, and that the movement has not addressed power differentials—which express themselves in terms of race and class—within itself and larger society in a sustained manner.[36] We would argue that without directly tackling class and race, what Phyllis Tickle has called "the great emergence" will be merely another novel idea that will ultimately benefit those who already reap plenty from the status quo. A concern for the postmodern world in which we live also needs to be tempered by a concern for the postcolonial world. The church of the multitude must be more intentional in bringing in the concerns of those who are at the bottom of society and the tensions between the 99 percent and the 1 percent.

A FORETASTE OF GOD'S REIGN

The assembly or gathering of the people of God is important because we do not live as autonomous, individualistic, and isolated selves. We depend on others for our existence, and we live and grow in community. Rita Nakashima Brock affirms that the Christian community is an incarnated body to continue the movement that Jesus started. She compares the work of the Christian community to that of the living transmission of Buddhism. It is through a teacher and a *sangha* (community) that the *dharma* (teaching) is transmitted, and not through individual study or reflection.[37] Similarly, we cannot come to understand the work of God and of Jesus Christ alone, but only through living in community and working together in service and in love.

A very important lesson we have learned from the Occupy movement is that we cannot ask people to believe that another world is possible without creating an environment where people can have a moment to experience and live into it. If the church of the multitude is to proclaim the good news of the coming or inbreaking of God's reign, it must provide the environment for people to have a foretaste of it. For instance, if the church is to proclaim that God's grace is inclusive and open to all, the church cannot discriminate against people because of skin color, financial status, sexual orientation, or immigrant status. Moreover, it needs to address the forces of oppression that encourage discrimination, including the class struggle, of which the Occupy movement has reminded us so powerfully.

Unfortunately, many of the church models and ways of organizing Christian communities that we have inherited are outdated and do not live up to the demands of the reign of God. This is particularly problematic in churches that still assume a "Christendom" mentality. One of the keenest critics of this Christendom mentality is British theologian Stuart Murray, who comes from the Anabaptist tradition that has existed on the margins of the established organization of the Church of England. Stuart Murray defines Christendom as the creation and maintenance of a Christian nation by forging a strong and close relationship between the Christian church and its host culture.[38] The Christendom mentality can be seen in a commitment to the hierarchy and status quo; a church at the center of society rather than the margins; a reliance on the clergy rather than lay involvement; a marginalization of women, the poor, and lesbian, gay, bisexual, and transgender people; the use of political forces to suppress dissident movements; and the alignment of the church's interests with the rich and the powerful.[39]

In order for the church to dissociate from the power and privilege associated with Christendom and its imperial approaches to church and mission, Murray exhorts the church to move from the center to the margins and to transition from a position of control to a position of witness. This means that we have to reimagine the incarnated body of Christ in new ways, such that it will not mirror the dominant society but will rather allow people to have a foretaste of and to live in anticipation of the reign of God. The body of Christ, as we have said in chapter 4, does not imply an organic hierarchy with the head over the body. The Pauline metaphor of the body of Christ is used to subvert the hierarchical system and to emphasize the interconnection among all the parts. If we use the model of the starfish to imagine the body, we will see more clearly that, as Paul has noted, the body is one and has many members (1 Cor. 12:12). The members need to coordinate with one another for the organism to move and function. This decentralized model is not leaderless, as we have seen in the Occupy movement, but "leaderfull," because many more people will be motivated to take responsibility and assume leadership. And, going beyond the image of the starfish, we are finding that the marginalized are playing special roles.

This implies an open invitation to all members of the body of Christ to participate in ministry, instead of limiting ministry to the clergy, religious professionals, and a group of privileged lay members. William Countryman, in his book *Living on the Border of the Holy*, begins a discussion of priesthood not from the ordained ministry, but from the ministry we offer to one another as human beings. We find his discussion particularly helpful because he defines priesthood and ministry in everyday life and in those acts of service we render to each other. He writes, "All human beings, knowingly or not, minister as priest to one another."[40] He includes work such as teaching, parenting, mentoring, and coaching as fulfilling this priestly function. The priesthood of Jesus, he reminds us, is not limited to his death and resurrection, but encompasses his whole life, in his daily working and mingling with all sorts of people. Countryman understands Jesus's ministry this way:

> It is a ministry that constantly transgresses boundaries. He teaches the crowds as well as the disciples. He engages in conversation with complete strangers. He heals indiscriminately, sometimes without being asked. His fellowship includes the impure. He crosses the line that separated Jew from Gentile.[41]

It is this model of self-giving ministry to others that the priesthood of the people of God is called to follow. The notion of priesthood cannot be narrowly defined as someone serving in a sanctuary and performing certain religious rites. Priesthood is serving others in our daily lives so that others may experience the presence and blessings of God. Countryman continues, "The primary Christian priesthood, like the fundamental priesthood of all humanity, belongs to the sphere of everyday human activity. It is not divorced from the profane world; it stands in the center of it."[42] We agree with Countryman that Christian priesthood takes place in our everyday lives, and we want to push further for a more blurred line between the holy and the profane, as described in his book. We see priesthood more in terms of functional leadership, and priests as people who fulfill particular roles and responsibilities in the community. Using the model of the starfish, priests can be seen as catalysts to gather people together, to help them form fellowship, and to plan actions for mission.

Through worship and rituals, the people of God can have a foretaste of the reign of God. The word "liturgy" in Greek originally meant "public service" or "the work of the people." But there is still very little involvement of people in liturgical acts apart from acting in predetermined ways. According to Rita Nakashima Brock, the liturgy of the mainline denominations is stale. She opines, "Worship in mainline denominations is anti-sensual and boring, because it does not engage the multiple forms of the senses. As a result, it does not engage the whole range of human beings and affection. The theology manifested in our worship is so outdated. The music is Eurocentric and mostly appeals to the geriatric members."[43]

The dissatisfaction with the liturgy is especially felt among women, who have been pushing the church to change for decades, ever since the women's movement began. While some have decided to leave the church altogether, many others remain and have developed an amazing wealth of liturgical materials and distinct women-identified rites. Teresa Berger, who has collected and studied these liturgies in a global context, attributes the emergence of such rites to lack of attention to the "gendered nature of worship practices to the church,"[44] such that different genders are supposed to play certain roles based on societal norms. Even though there have been different waves of liturgical renewal of worship life in various denominations, women's experiences have been either left out or not fully included. The liturgical renewal also has not responded to the tremendous cultural shift that changed the position of women in the latter half of the twentieth century. As an alternative, women have developed, created, and passed on women's rites used in women's groups, adult forums, women's retreats, divinity schools, ecumenical gatherings, and a range of both ecclesial and non-ecclesial settings. These women-identified liturgies represent a historical process that Berger has called "the 'irruption' of women in the world of ritual."[45] These liturgies use local resources and yet have transnational linkages because of growing feminist networks across the globe. They are often more than the product of one

single individual, are created communally, and respond to particular contexts
and needs. Berger notes, "What emerges from the stories of these communities and their ritualizing is remarkably close to the characteristics of what
has been called theologies of the people."[46] It is through ritualizing that
women express their theology in embodied ways that enrich their own lives
and empower the communities.

We would like to cite two examples of these women-identified rituals
from the opening and closing rituals of the annual meeting held in March
2012 of Pacific, Asian, and North American Asian Women in Theology and
Ministry. Each participant in the meeting was asked to bring three ounces of
water from a source of nature near her home. During the opening ceremony,
the altar was decorated with colorful cloths, stones, and flowers, and a large
crystal bowl was placed on it. Each participant was asked to introduce herself, say something about the source of the water and her expectations and
hopes for the meeting, and then pour her water in the crystal bowl. This was a
powerful experience, for each had a chance to share stories of joy and struggles; one participant even said she had thought of offering three ounces of
her own tears. Then, during the closing ritual, each participant came forward
to say what the meeting had meant for her and to wash her hands in the bowl
of water, remaining there until the next person came to the altar. The next
person would use a towel to dry her sister's hands. That was repeated until all
had their turn. Grace Yia-Hei Kao, who participated in this meeting, describes what these rituals meant for her: "I loved the highlighting of individual experience and corporate togetherness, the juxtaposition of solemnity and
comedy, and the sharing of trials and triumphs. I also loved how the drying
of hands [with the towel] conjured images of Jesus' washing of his disciples'
feet."[47] Such inspiring rituals have been created in many Asian and Asian
American women's meetings, using Asian and Asian American religious and
cultural elements to express their identities. These rituals empower women to
build communal bonds in the struggle against the patriarchal churches and
society that marginalize their ministries.

Rituals and symbolic actions are important ways to cultivate a different
way of being in the world and of relating to one another. Rituals that rein-
scribe the power differentials of the world would likely cultivate habits of
thoughts and behaviors that reinforce the status quo. Rituals that subvert
power and disrupt our common sense would more likely bring us to the
liminal spaces, which are spaces in between, that Victor Turner has described
in his study of the ritual process.[48] In these liminal spaces, participants are

able to think of their roles anew because they are in transition between what is familiar and what is yet to come. Marcella Althaus-Reid argues that rituals should disrupt the power dynamics of society, and she brings her feminist liberation critique to bear on how the Eucharist is celebrated in the Latin American context. She observes the alienation of the product of the bread from the producers, who are usually women, when the bread needs to go through intermediaries or distribution by the male priests. The Eucharistic act in and of itself, if it is based on an exclusively male priesthood, will not redistribute power and privilege, but will instead reinforce them. Althaus-Reid asks us to imagine how women, the poor, and sexual minorities can have a voice in what she calls "a divine redistributional, sacrament act of power."[49] She continues, "Sacraments are more than enclosed encounters with God: they act as ways of understanding love, or even ways of having voices of protest symbolically heard."[50] If these kinds of rituals and sacraments are available to the multitude, the multitude will not be passive recipients of divine grace. They will instead be nurtured by a *habitus* of resistance, which will make them productive agents to carry out God's mission because they will have a foretaste of the fullness of God's blessings, which we refer to as God's shalom.

WITNESSING GOD'S SHALOM

The Hebrew word "shalom" is usually translated as "peace." But in the translation process, we have lost some of the important theological and ethical dimensions that define "shalom." Peace does not mean the absence of violence or war, and it cannot be reduced to a certain sense of equilibrium, avoidance of conflict, and the maintenance of the status quo. Bruce Ellis Benson, Malinda Elizabeth Berry, and Peter Goodwin Heltzel helpfully remind us that when Jesus said, "Peace I leave with you; my peace I give it to you. I do not give to you as the world gives" (John 14:27), Jesus contrasted God's peace with that of the world. "God calls us to *shalom*," they continue, "the biblical peace that is concerned with justice, equity, and integrity—what we do and the kind of people we strive to be."[51]

As long as we allow the cultural logic of the 1 percent to run the world and condemn the vast majority of the world's people to struggle for survival, there will be no peace. For we must recognize that terror and violence already exist, even though there may seemingly be peace and the absence of war on the surface. To achieve shalom, we must remove the root causes of injustice and restore just relationships among people. The World Council of Churches uses the term "just-peace" to describe the inseparable relation between justice and peace. Indeed, the psalmist has said, "Steadfast love and faithfulness will meet; righteousness and peace will kiss each other" (Ps. 85:10). The Hebrew prophets have spoken about restoring peace to the land and to the poor. They emphasize that the land belongs to God and is not owned by us (Ps. 24:1). In this sense, we are all "occupiers" because land is a gift from God, and we have to learn to live with creation and to share its bounty with others.

The work of God's shalom is not easy, for it involves working across differences. The proclamation of shalom to the world will become empty words if the communities of faith have not learned to embody shalom in their communal lives. We should have no illusions that the coming together of the multitude will be an easy process without conflicts and challenges. In the Occupy campsites, conflicts occurred among people with different backgrounds and diverse interests. The protest chaplains and others had to stop fights and help people to listen to each other. People who were passionate about justice could be impatient and self-righteous with others. There were people who wanted to use the name of the Occupy movement to do things that might not benefit the whole. Others wanted to dominate even in a leaderless movement where leadership was supposed to be shared. But the horizontal, self-organizing mode of leadership appears to have more potential than top-down leadership dominated by a few. Without attending to the process of how the multitude relate to each other, there will not be long-lasting peace. In the struggles for independence from colonialism, we have seen revolutionaries turn into dictators and tyrants when they assumed absolute power.

Working for shalom requires attention to cultural and religious differences in genuine ways. For Christians, we have much to learn, since the history of Christianity has been so enmeshed with colonial enterprises like the Crusades, the conquest of the Americas, the colonization of Africa and Asia, and the suppression of other cultures and religions. Many Christians believe there is one God, one faith, and one truth. But truth is not something we possess; rather, it is to be discovered in dialogues with one another and in working together in deep solidarity. Some theologians have begun to develop the notion of *polydoxy*, which implies many paths to truth, to describe both the internal diversity within the Christian tradition and the plurality of the religious traditions of humankind.[52] The intolerance of diversity, the suppression of dissident voices, and the expulsion of so-called heretics within the Christian tradition have become a model for intolerance and suppression of other cultures and religions when powerful empires rule over colonized peoples. Polydoxy embraces diversity so that it is possible not only to see one's own tradition through others' eyes but also to embrace one's own tradition more faithfully and to construct it anew where necessary. As Jewish educator Jared Cass said during an interfaith dialogue, we impoverish ourselves if we do not know other traditions. [53]

Polydoxy is rooted in the encounter of plurality of the divine and the cosmos all around us. Just as without biodiversity the whole planet cannot survive, without plurality the people of God and the work for shalom will be greatly diminished. For Brazilian ecofeminist theologian Ivone Gebara, trinity expresses this plurality because it symbolizes the interrelatedness, communion, and reciprocity of all life in a continuous and dynamic process of creativity. She beautifully describes how in the cosmos, trinity manifests as multiplicity and interdependence of the stars and galaxies. On earth, trinity is shown in the interconnectedness of all life forms and the movement toward cosmic citizenship on earth, beyond the confines of national boundaries and particular locale. [54] We venture to say that trinity is also manifested in the deep solidarity when the multitude work together to witness God's shalom.

Participating in the Occupy movement, Christians are learning new ways to work with many people of other religious faiths and of no faith for the common goal of bringing about justice and solidarity. Rosaries and candles of Mary of Guadalupe are placed next to images of Gandhi, John Lennon, and the Buddha and objects of nature such as stones, flowers, and seashells on the altars in open spaces and in the faith and spirituality tents. Christianity is brought to the public square not to dominate but as one religious tradition of humankind and one strand among the many. It is only through respecting the integrity and the otherness of the other that dialogue can truly happen and the work of deep solidarity can begin. In the public ritual during the Occupy Faith National Gathering at Oakland, California, leaders of different religious traditions were asked to contribute something from their traditions in which others could participate. The goal was not to produce something artificial, but to respect the specificities of each tradition.

Working with others in deep solidarity helps us understand difference in embodied ways when we stand shoulder to shoulder for justice in social movements for women's rights; the environment; the rights of lesbian, gay, bisexual, and transgender people; the rights of working people and the poor;

and the rights of the physically challenged. CB Stewart, a Judson Memorial Church community minister, helped organize interfaith services at Zuccotti Park with her friends. As a white queer person, she said that she likes to organize people who are like her, who have the same values and similar class backgrounds. But the experience of working with so many different people in the Occupy movement helped her to see that she had to "move beyond ethical commonality to intersectional movement building that is at the point of survival."[55] This was hard work, she said. Yet people were able to connect with each other in rhizomatic ways, horizontally in many directions, in what was a messy, heterogeneous organizational structure.

The work for shalom requires us to go beyond our narrow definitions of tribe, race, and religion in order to work for the benefit of the 99 percent. At the height of the civil rights movement, some people wondered why the Rev. Martin Luther King Jr. would connect civil rights with the war in Vietnam. In a sermon King preached at Riverside Church in New York in 1967, he linked the plight of the poor and African Americans in the United States with the suffering of Vietnamese people and appealed to his fellow Americans to stop the war. He said, "All life is interrelated. We are caught in an inescapable network of mutuality, tied into a single garment of destiny."[56] In his sermon, he referenced messages from Vietnamese Buddhist leaders and tapped into the liberative resources of religion. He concluded, "When I speak of love, I am not speaking of some sentimental weak response. I am speaking of that force which all great religions have seen as the supreme unifying principle of life. Love is somehow the key that unlocks the door which leads to ultimate reality."[57]

Religious faith can be a powerful force in social movements, as sociologist Christian Smith described in *Disruptive Religion*. Religion can provide the legitimation for protest based on its understanding of the ultimate or sacred, and it can provide moral imperatives for love, justice, peace, and equity. Its rituals, symbols, songs, and testimonies, which help to shape collective identities, express grievances, and provide inspirations, can be put to use for political mobilization. Religion also provides organizational resources, such as trained and experienced leadership, congregated participants, and preexisting networks.[58] CB Stewart maintained that she was able to use what she learned in church to participate in the Occupy movement. She said traditional rituals create space to mark and lift up passages of life—birth, marriage, dying—and allow people and the congregation to move slowly through time and space. The Judson Memorial Church was able to contribute to Occupy Wall Street by helping people to move slowly through ritual time and channel their energy for the creation of counterpower. Out of that ritual experience, people could respond more imaginatively. [59]

The liberating potential of holding ritual in public space was keenly felt in the Kol Nidre service held at Yom Kippur in New York. Getzel Davis, a rabbinic student in Boston, and his friends helped to organize the ritual. They used the traditional liturgy, while adding prayers used in progressive Jewish groups. For him, it was extremely moving that Jewish people were able to express their faith openly in public in support of the Occupy movement. [60] Yom Kippur was an especially powerful occasion because it is the time when Jews renew their relationship with God and commit to work for justice. During the service, they were reminded of what the prophet Isaiah said:

> "Is such the fast that I choose," says the voice of God, "a day to humble oneself? Is it to bow down the head like a bulrush, and to lie in sackcloth and ashes? Will you call this a fast, a day acceptable to the Lord? Is not this the fast that I choose: to loose the bonds of injustice, to undo the thongs of the yoke, to let the oppressed go free, and to break every yoke? Is it not to share your bread with the hungry, and bring the homeless poor into your house; when you see the naked, to cover them, and not to hide yourself from your own kin?" (58: 5–7)

Worship has nothing to do with passive reception of the divine or with narrow religious ritual. Worship, as we understand the prophet Isaiah and the tradition in which he stands, has to do with the production of justice. In his sermon at the service, Davis said that it was easy to confuse gold and God, and he spoke of the golden calf as a paradigmatic example of that. He warned against the orientation of one's life solely around the acquisition of money, which he connected to worship of the golden calf. He concluded by saying that "service to humankind is sacred and a reflection of service to God,"[61] and his words were made even more powerful because people repeated what he said by using the people's microphone. Many felt the service was deeply moving and empowering, especially toward the end of the service when people were asked to name what they were committed to do. The service was radical "because Jews have not done so in public in a ritual manner," Davis said.

As we conclude this book, we are very grateful to the people with whom we have worked and whom we have interviewed because their work for shalom and commitment to justice inspired us, and we recommit ourselves to our own work for justice and peace. The Rev. Edmund Harris has decided to start an outdoor church for homeless people in Providence, Rhode Island, and is raising funds for this project. CB Stewart is preparing for ordained ministry in the United Church of Christ to continue doing just-peace work. Getzel Davis is training to become a rabbi and will continue to be involved in different progressive movements because, for him, religion and politics cannot be separated. Rita Nakashima Brock will start a center and help create a new field to study the moral injuries of veterans. In Dallas, the work on religion and labor continues in what is one of the most difficult places for labor in the country. It is from our encounters with people and our involvement with projects like these that we continue to learn what "occupy religion" means. We remain hopeful for God's shalom.

Epilogue

A theology of the multitude is never finished. This is due to its bottom-up character and the complexity of the task. Because a theology of the multitude unfolds in movements of people encountering the movements of the divine along the way, no one person or group can ever be in control of it, and no theologian can ever exhaust it.

Many of our religious traditions unfolded in this bottom-up way as well. The Jewish traditions to which the Christian and Muslim traditions are indebted are inextricably related to liberation movements of slaves and people in exile. Many of our sacred texts, including the New Testament, are witnesses to the diversity of movements that gave birth to the Christian traditions. This is why there are four different gospels and a diversity of authors, some not even known by name. These movements are held together by their witness to the liberative work of Jesus Christ on the margins of the Roman Empire and the alternative ways of life that sprang from it.

For all these reasons, we are not claiming to have produced *the* theology of the multitude. But we are also not offering merely *a* theology of the multitude that can be shelved as just another consumer product. The theology of the multitude presented here takes seriously the movements of the Spirit in the world today. The Occupy movement is one example of such a movement of the Spirit. It brings together many of the concerns of liberation movements of the past and adds a clearer understanding of where the tensions are in a globalizing world dominated by neoliberal capitalism and the interests of the 1 percent. Most importantly, the Occupy movement gives new energy to what we are calling deep solidarity.

The solidarity of the 99 percent reminds us that many more of us are in the same boat than we ever suspected. And it affords us fresh insights into the movements of the divine and of the many communities that are inspired by them. This solidarity of the multitude does not demand uniformity; on the contrary, it thrives on diversity, and also encourages it. Even the 1 percent are invited to join, and a few have accepted this invitation. The common cause is now clearer than ever before: perhaps for the first time in history, not only do we have to consider seriously the survival of the marginalized majority, but we also have to consider the survival of humanity and the planet as a whole if wealth and power are increasingly monopolized for the benefit of fewer and fewer people.

The unfinished character of a theology of the multitude in the midst of these struggles is a sign of hope. Most of the finished theologies of empire, which have ruled supreme for certain times, have already met their demise. And the ones still in effect will not last forever. An unfinished theology serves as a constant reminder that things do not have to be as they are at the moment. The hope of a theology of the multitude is not the sort of hope that makes people buy lottery tickets or believe in pie-in-the-sky dreams or Ponzi schemes that never materialize. The hope that we are talking about is embodied in movements that are transforming the world and in a God who is drawing closer to the humanity of the 99 percent than any of the elites could ever hope to be. We invite you to participate in developing theology of multitude through concrete reflection and action.

Notes

1. WHY OCCUPY RELIGION?

1. Huffington Post, *OCCUPY: Why It Started. Who's Behind It. What's Next* (Kindle Location 271). Huffington Post Media Group. Kindle Edition.

2. Andy Kroll, "How Occupy Wall Street Really Got Started," in *This Changes Everything: Occupy Wall Street and the 99% Movement*, ed. Sarah van Gelder and the staff of *YES!* magazine (San Francisco: Berrett-Koehler, 2011), 16–21.

3. "The Protesters," *Time*, www.time.com/time/person-of-the-year/2011 (accessed January 14, 2012).

4. Occupy Wall Street, "2011: A Year in Revolt," http://occupywallst.org/article/2011-year-revolt (posted January 3, 2012).

5. Brian Stelter, "Camps Are Clear, But '99 Percent' Still Occupies the Lexicon," *New York Times*, www.nytimes.com/2011/12/01/us/we-are-the-99-percent-joins-the-cultural-and-political-lexicon.html (accessed April 5, 2012).

6. Three theologians, Gustavo Gutiérrez in Latin America, and James Cone and Frederick Herzog in the United States, came up with the term "liberation theology" independent of each other and published initial books and articles without knowing that others had used this term at the same time.

7. For a fresh take on the understanding of class from a theological perspective, see Joerg Rieger, *No Rising Tide: Theology, Economics, and the Future* (Minneapolis: Fortress Press, 2009).

8. Max Weber, *From Max Weber: Essays in Sociology*, trans. Hans Heinrich Gerth and C. Wright Mills (New York: Oxford University Press, 1946), 155.

9. Michael E. Agnes, ed., *Webster's New World College Dictionary*, 4th ed. (Indianapolis: Wiley, 2004).

10. In Nazi Germany, for instance, the churches that withdrew from public life in order to practice their religion in what they considered nonpolitical fashion realized too late that their withdrawal amounted to a tacit support of the system.

11. Michael Hardt and Antonio Negri, *Empire* (Cambridge, MA: Harvard University Press, 2000), xii.

12. Michael Hardt and Antonio Negri, *Multitude: War and Democracy in the Age of Empire* (New York: Penguin, 2004), 15.

13. Kwok Pui-lan, Don H. Compier, and Joerg Rieger, eds., *Empire and the Christian Tradition: New Readings of Classical Theologians* (Minneapolis: Fortress Press, 2007).

2. WE ARE THE 99 PERCENT

1. See http://wearethe99percent.tumblr.com/Introduction (accessed April 5, 2012).

2. Sarah van Gelder, "How Occupy Wall Street Changes Everything," in *This Changes Everything: Occupy Wall Street and the 99 % Movement*, ed. Sarah van Gelder and the staff of *YES!* magazine (San Francisco: Berrett-Koehler, 2011), 1.

3. Michael Scherer, "Taking It to the Streets," *Time*, October 24, 2011, 23. The percentages are taken from a *Time*/Abt SRIBI poll, *Time*, October 24, 2011, 22.

4. Joerg Rieger discusses this logic in both its economic and religious forms in his book *No Rising Tide: Theology, Economics, and the Future* (Minneapolis: Fortress Press, 2009).

5. "First Communiqué: We Occupy Wall Street," posted by OccupyWallSt, September 19, 2011, in *Voices from the 99 Percent: An Oral History of the Occupy Wall Street Movement*, ed. Lenny Flank (St. Petersburg, FL: Red and Black, 2011), 24.

6. "IWW General Defense Committee Statement in Support of Occupy Wall Street," September 28, 2011, in *Voices from the 99 Percent*, 53.

7. Sabrina Tavernise, "Rich-Poor Gap Seen as Top U.S. Clash," *Dallas Morning News*, January 12, 2012, 6A. The perception of class conflict surged most among white, middle-income earners. At the same time, the belief in upward mobility has not changed, and 43 percent believe that the rich are wealthy because of "their own hard work, ambition or education." This number has remained constant since 2008.

8. Hannah Hofheinz, "Occupy Privilege," paper presented at the panel on "Occupy@AAR/SBL" at the annual meeting of the American Academy of Religion and Society of Biblical Literature, San Francisco, November 20, 2011.

9. On October 19, 2011, the *Wall Street Journal* posted a percentage calculator titled "What Percentage Are You?" http://blogs.wsj.com/economics/2011/10/19/what-percent-are-you/?mod=wsj_share_facebook&mid=549 (accessed December 7, 2011).

10. Joseph E. Stiglitz, "Of the 1%, by the 1%, for the 1%," *Vanity Fair*, May 2011, www.vanityfair.com/society/features/2011/05/top-one-percent-201105 (accessed April 4, 2012).

11. These numbers have been verified by PolitiFact, as seen at www.politifact.com/wisconsin/statements/2011/mar/10/michael-moore/michael-moore-says-400-americans-have-more-wealth-/ (accessed December 7, 2011).

12. These numbers are from a report by the Economic Policy Institute. See Sylvia A. Alegretto, "The State of Working America's Wealth, 2011," EPI Briefing Paper no. 292 (March 23, 2011), 7, http://epi.3cdn.net/2a7ccb3e9e618f0bbc_3nm6idnax.pdf (accessed December 7, 2011).

13. Jared Bernstein, "Inequality Growing, and Government Doing Less about It," Center on Budget and Policy Priorities, October 27, 2011, www.offthechartsblog.org/inequality-growing-and-government-doing-less-about-it (accessed December 7, 2011).

14. Annalyn Censky, "A Rough Ten Years for the Middle Class," *CNN Money*, October 14, 2011, http://money.cnn.com/2011/09/21/news/economy/middle_class_income/index.htm (accessed April 6, 2012).

15. See Michael Moore, "The Purpose of Occupy Wall Street Is to Occupy Wall Street," *Nation of Change*, March 18, 2012, www.nationofchange.org/purpose-occupy-wall-street-occupy-wall-street-1332087679 (accessed April 22, 2012).

16. "US Wealth Gap Widens between the Races," *News24*, July 26, 2011, www.news24.com/World/News/US-wealth-gap-widens-between-races-20110726 (accessed April 6, 2012).

17. "Urban League: Black Middle Class Losing Ground," *USA Today*, July 27, 2011, www.usatoday.com/news/nation/2011-07-27-black-middle-class-study_n.htm.

18. Robert Reich, "Whose Recovery?" *Nation of Change*, March 31, 2012, www.nationofchange.org/whose-recovery-1333202811 (accessed April 22, 2012).

19. Max Fisher, "Map: U.S. Ranks Near Bottom on Income Inequality," *Atlantic*, September 19, 2011, www.theatlantic.com/international/archive/2011/09/map-us-ranks-near-bottom-on-income-inequality/245315 (accessed December 7, 2011).

20. Already in the 1990s, when the global victory of capitalism was declared, the global market no longer benefited the workforce of the so-called First World automatically, as it had done for some time. See William Wolman and Anne Colamosca, *The Judas Economy: The Triumph of Capital and the Betrayal of Work* (Reading, MA: AddisonWesley, 1997).

21. "Record 48% Considered Low-Income," *Dallas Morning News*, December 15, 2011, 7A. The low-income threshold is $45,000 for a family of four. A total of 97.3 million Americans are considered low income (earning between 100 and 199 percent of the poverty level), while 49.1 million are below the poverty line. This number adds up to 146.4 million Americans, or 48 percent of the population. Most children are likely to be poor or low income: 57 percent. Hispanics: 73 percent. Twenty-nine U.S. cities report that one in four people needing emergency food assistance did not receive it.

22. "We are the 1 percent. We stand with the 99 percent," http://westandwith-the99percent.tumblr.com (accessed December 7, 2011).

23. "Billionaire George Soros: I Should Pay More in Taxes," *Thinkprogress*, comment posted February 13, 2012, http://thinkprogress.org/economy/2012/02/13/424000/soros-pay-more-taxes/?mobile=nc (accessed April 6, 2012).

24. In a case before the Michigan Supreme Court in 1919 (*Dodge v. Ford Motor Company*), the brothers John Francis Dodge and Horace Elgin Dodge, owners of 10 percent of Ford stock, challenged Ford's decision to cut dividends in order to invest in new plants and grow production and numbers of workers while cutting prices. The court ruled in favor of the Dodge brothers, arguing that a corporation is organized primarily for the profit of its stockholders, rather than for the benefit of its employees or for the community. See the brief entry in Wikipedia, "Dodge v. Ford Motor Company," http://en.wikipedia.org/wiki/Dodge_v._Ford_Motor_Company (accessed December 7, 2011).

25. "CHARTS: Here Is What the Wall Street Protesters Are So Angry About . . ." *Business Insider*, October 11, 2011, www.businessinsider.com/what-wall-street-protesters-are-so-angry-about-2011-10?op=1 (accessed April 6, 2012).

26. In 2006, the average CEO made 364 times more than an average worker in the United States. However, there is another number that is perhaps more telling and much less known. The difference between the salary of an average worker and the salary of the top twenty private-equity and hedge-fund managers in the United States is in a different league altogether: on average, members of this latter group earned 22,255 times the pay of the average worker.

Sarah Anderson et al., *Executive Excess 2007: The Staggering Social Cost of U.S. Business Leadership* (Washington, DC: Institute for Policy Studies and United for a Fair Economy, 2007), 9, www.ips-dc.org/reports/070829-executiveexcess.pdf (accessed December 7, 2011).

27. "International Comparisons of Trade Unions," Wikipedia, http://en.wikipedia.org/wiki/International_comparisons_of_labor_unions (accessed April 6, 2012).

28. For some of the unemployment statistics that back up these numbers, see "Alternate Unemployment Charts," in John Williams's Shadow Government Statistics website, www.shadowstats.com/alternate_data/unemployment-charts (accessed December 7, 2011).

29. There is a lot more to be said about the reality of the working class. See, for instance, the studies that are done under the heading "New Working-Class Studies," such as John Russo and Sherry Lee Linkon, eds., *New Working-Class Studies* (Ithaca, NY: ILR, 2005).

30. Joerg Rieger has begun to use this term recently; see Joerg Rieger, "Occupy Wall Street and Everything Else: Lessons for the Study and Praxis of Religion," *Peace Studies Journal* 5, no. 1 (January 2012): 33–45, http://peaceconsortium.org/wp-content/uploads/2010/01/PSJ-Rieger-33-45.pdf.

31. Andy Kroll, "How Occupy Wall Street Really Got Started," in *This Changes Everything*, 20.

32. "Declaration of the Occupation of New York City," September 29, 2011, in *Voices from the 99 Percent*, 55.

33. "Call for #GlobalSpring for #GlobalChange," *InterOccupy*, February 8, 2012, http://interoccupy.org/globalspring (accessed April 7, 2012).

34. William I. Robinson and Jerry Harris, "Towards a Global Ruling Class: Globalization and the Transnational Capitalist Class," *Science & Society* 64, no. 1 (Spring 2000): 11–54, http://net4dem.org/mayglobal/Papers/RobinsonHarris7_16.pdf (accessed April 7, 2012).

35. For the ongoing importance of the nation-state, see Ellen Meiksins Wood, *The Empire of Capital* (London: Verso, 2003).

36. Charles Duhigg and Keith Bradsher, "How the U.S. Lost Out on iPhone Work," *New York Times*, January 22, 2012, www.nytimes.com/2012/01/22/business/apple-america-and-a-squeezed-middle-class.html?pagewanted=all (accessed April 7, 2012).

37. Ben Blanchard, "Apple, Foxconn Scandal Highlights Exploitation of Chinese Workers by Foreign Firms," *Huffington Post*, comment posted March 7, 2012, www.huffingtonpost.com/2012/03/07/apple-foxconn-scandal_n_1325930.html (accessed April 7, 2012).

38. Saskia Sassen, *Globalization and Its Discontents: Essays on the New Mobility of People and Money* (New York: New Press, 1998), 111–31.

39. Will Deener, "Working?" *Dallas Morning News*, July 13, 2009, 4D.

40. Puleng LenkaBula, "Justice and Fullness of Life in the Context of Economic Globalization: An African Woman's Perspective," *Reformed World* 52, no. 4 (2002): 163–74. For a discussion of how globalization affects Third World women, see Kwok Pui-lan, "Introduction," in *Hope Abundant: Third World and Indigenous Women's Theology* (Maryknoll, NY: Orbis Books, 2011), 2–6.

41. Douglas Kellner, "Preemptive Strikes and the War on Iraq: A Critique of Bush Administration Unilateralism and Militarism," http://pages.gseis.ucla.edu/faculty/kellner/essays/preemptivestrikesoniraq.pdf (accessed April 8, 2012).

42. Christina Lin, "The New Silk Road: China's Energy Strategy in the Greater Middle East—The Four Seas Strategy," *Cutting Edge*, May 28, 2011, www.thecuttingedgenews.com/index.php?article=52075&pageid=&pagename (accessed April 9, 2012).

43. *Time* magazine, *What Is Occupy? Inside the Global Movement* (New York: Time Books, 2011), 62–63.

44. Leslie Sklair, *The Transnational Capitalist Class* (Malden, MA: Blackwell, 2001), 6.

45. For a more detailed analysis, see Rieger, *No Rising Tide*, chap. 4.

46. See, for example, Laurie Beth Jones, *Jesus, CEO: Using Ancient Wisdom for Visionary Leadership* (New York: Hyperion, 1995).

47. See, for instance, Joerg Rieger's reflections on the ancient confession that Jesus is Lord in *Christ and Empire: From Paul to Postcolonial Times* (Minneapolis: Fortress Press, 1997), chap. 1.

48. This is one of the key questions that Latin American liberation theology has raised, most recently by Jung Mo Sung in *The Subject, Capitalism, and Religion: Horizons of Hope in Complex Societies* (New York: Palgrave Macmillan, 2011).

49. A well-known example is the Mondragon Corporation, a Spanish federation of worker cooperatives that are owned by their workers and governed democratically. At present, it is the seventh-largest Spanish company, employing more than eighty-thousand people at the end of 2010. For more information, see www.justpeace.org/mondragon.htm (accessed December 7, 2011).

50. Hamil R. Harris, "Growing Number of African American Pastors Express Support for Occupy Movement," *Washington Post*, January 20, 2012, www.washingtonpost.com/local/african-american-pastors-express-support-for-occupy-movement/2012/01/18/gIQAyofFEQ_story.html?tid=pm_local_pop (accessed April 22, 2012). The pastors included the Rev. Carroll A. Baltimore Sr., president of the Progressive National Baptist Convention.

51. See the various websites of Occupyfaith: http://occupyfaithnyc.com and www.occupyfaith.com. The website of the protest chaplains is also noteworthy: http://protestchaplains.blogspot.com.

3. THE MULTITUDE SPRINGS INTO ACTION

1. The quotes are from a personal reflection written by Brendan Curran, used by permission. Curran was interviewed in Boston on January 11, 2012.

2. Gary Dorrien, "The Case against Wall Street: Why the Protesters Are Angry," *Christian Century*, November 15, 2011, 22.

3. Michael Hardt and Antonio Negri, *Commonwealth* (Cambridge, MA: Harvard University Press, 2009), 169.

4. Francis Fukuyama, *The End of History and the Last Man* (New York: Free Press, 1992).

5. Joseph E. Stiglitz, *Globalization and Its Discontents* (New York: W. W. Norton, 2003), 214.

6. Ben Blanchard, "Apple, Foxconn Scandal Highlights Exploitation of Chinese Workers by Foreign Firms," *Huffington Post*, comment posted March 7, 2012, www.huffingtonpost.com/2012/03/07/apple-foxconn-scandal_n_1325930.html (accessed March 24, 2012).

7. Arjun Appadurai, "Grassroots Globalization and the Research Imagination," in *Globalization*, ed. Arjun Appadurai (Durham, NC: Duke University Press, 2001), 1–21. For an assessment of how the Christian traditions related to globalization from above and globalization from below, see Joerg Rieger, *Globalization and Theology: Horizons in Theology* (Nashville, TN: Abingdon Press, 2010).

8. Appadurai, "Grassroots Globalization," 3.

9. Sarah van Gelder, "How Occupy Wall Street Changes Everything," in *This Changes Everything: Occupy Wall Street and the 99% Movement*, ed. Sarah van Gelder and the staff of *YES!* magazine (San Francisco: Berrett-Koehler, 2011), 6.

10. Sermon by John Allen, used by permission.

11. On February 15, 2012, 99 Percent Spring was launched with support from over forty prominent national leaders and organizations; see http://the99spring.com/who-we-are (accessed May 2, 2012).

12. Marina Sitrin, "One No, Many Yesses," in *Occupy! Scenes from Occupied America*, ed. Astra Taylor et al. (New York: Verso, 2011), 8.

13. Judith Butler and Gayatri Chakravorty Spivak, *Who Sings the Nation-State?* (London: Seagull Books, 2010), 38–39.

14. Enrique Dussel, *Politics of Liberation: A Critical World History*, trans. Thia Cooper (London: SCM Press, 2011), xv.

15. Ibid., xvi.

16. Stephen Gandel, "The Leaders of a Leaderless Movement," in *What Is Occupy? Inside the Global Movement*, ed. *Time* magazine (New York: Time Books, 2011), 36.

17. Marina Sitrin, "Horizontalism: From Argentina to Wall Street," *NACLA Report on the Americas* 44, no. 6 (November/December 2011): 8.

18. Staughton Lynd and Andrej Grubacic, *Wobblies and Zapatistas: Conversations on Anarchism, Marxism and Radical History* (Oakland, CA: PM Press, 2008), 50.

19. Jennifer Wilder, personal interview, New York, April 17, 2012.

20. Micah L. Sifry, "@OccupyWallStreet: A Leaderfull Movement in a Leaderless Time," *TechPresident*, comment posted November 14, 2011, http://techpresident.com/blog-entry/occupywallstreet-leaderfull-movement-leaderless-time (accessed April 25, 2012).

21. Sally Quinn, "Cornel West Keeps the Faith for Occupy Wall Street," *Washington Post*, November 10, 2011, www.washingtonpost.com/blogs/on-faith/post/cornel-west-keeps-the-faith-for-occupy-wall-street/2011/11/10/gIQAZxhk8M_blog.html (accessed January 22, 2012).

22. Historian Lynn Hunt studied the political culture of the French revolution, and her insights are helpful for looking at the Occupy movement. See *Politics, Culture, and Class in the French Revolution* (Berkeley: University of California Press, 1984).

23. Butler and Spivak, *Who Sings the Nation-State?*, 26–27.

24. Ishaan Tharoor, "Hands Across the World," in *What Is Occupy?*, ed. *Time* magazine, 29.

25. Clay Shirky, *Here Comes Everybody: The Power of Organizing without Organizations* (New York: Penguin, 2009), 55.

26. Steven Johnson, *Emergence: The Connected Lives of Ants, Brains, Cities, and Software* (New York: Touchstone Books, 2001), 224.

27. Janell Ross and Trymaine Lee, "Occupy the Hood Aims to Draw People of Color to Wall Street," *Huffington Post*, comment posted October 14, 2011, www.huffingtonpost.com/2011/10/14/occupy-the-hood-occupy-wall-street_n_1009850.html (accessed April 26, 2012).

28. Michael Hardt and Antonio Negri, "What to Expect in 2012," *Adbusters*, December 8, 2011, www.adbusters.org/magazine/99/under-no-illusions.html (accessed April 26, 2012).

29. Tim Murphy, "Newt Gingrich to Occupiers: Take a Bath and Go Get a Job!" *Mother Jones*, November 2011, http://motherjones.com/mojo/2011/11/newt-gingrich-ows-take-bath (accessed January 22, 2012).

30. Jon Bershad, "Rush Limbaugh: Occupy Wall Street Protesters Probably Glad They Can Now 'Move Back In with Their Parents,'" Mediaite.com, November 16, 2011, http://www.mediaite.com/online/rush-limbaugh-occupy-wall-street-protesters-probably-glad-they-can-now-%E2%80%98move-back-in-with-their-parents%E2%80%99 (accessed January 22, 2012).

31. The quotes are taken from an exchange between David Brooks and Gail Collins, "Is Occupy Wall Street Overhyped?" *New York Times*, October 19, 2011, http://opinionator.blogs.nytimes.com/2011/10/19/is-occupy-wall-street-being-overhyped (accessed January 22, 2012).

32. Niall Ferguson, *Colossus: The Price of America's Empire* (New York: Penguin Books, 2004).

33. "Jeffrey Sachs vs. Niall Ferguson on the Occupy Wall Street Movement (CNN Video)," CNN, www.distressedvolatility.com/2011/11/jeffrey-sachs-vs-niall-ferguson-on.html (accessed January 22, 2012).

34. Angela Davis, "(Un)Occupy: Remarks at Washington Square Park, October 30," in *Occupy! Scenes from Occupied America*, ed. Astra Taylor et al., 133.

35. "Indians Counter Occupy Wall Street Movement with Decolonize Wall Street," *Live Leak*, October 6, 2011, www.liveleak.com/view?i=624_1318362167 (accessed April 27, 2012).

36. Hunt, *Politics, Culture, and Class*, 189–90.

37. Slavoj Žižek, "Don't Fall in Love with Yourselves: Remarks at Zuccotti Park, October 9," in *Occupy! Scenes from Occupied America*, ed. Astra Taylor et al., 69.

38. Ibid., 68–69.

39. Alan Rusbridger, "Canon of St. Paul: Church Cannot Answer Peaceful Protest with Violence," *Guardian*, October, 27, 2011, www.guardian.co.uk/uk/2011/oct/27/st-pauls-canon-occupy-london-camp (accessed January 23, 2012).

40. Rowan Williams, "Time for Us to Challenge the Idol of High Finance," *Financial Times*, November 1, 2011, www.ft.com/intl/cms/s/0/a561a4f6-0485-11e1-ac2a-00144feabdc0.html#axzz1tY9bD5fy (accessed April 30, 2012).

41. "A Message of Solidarity from the Archbishop Desmond Tutu," *Occupy Wall Street*, December 15, 2011, http://occupywallst.org/article/message-solidarity-archbishop-desmond-tutu (accessed January 23, 2012).

42. "Joan Baez Sings at Occupy Wall Street," YouTube, www.commondreams.org/video/2011/11/12 (accessed January 23, 2012).

43. Mike Conklin, "Can Miley Cyrus Really Further the Occupy Wall Street Cause?" *L Magazine*, November 28, 2011, www.thelmagazine.com/TheMeasure/archives/2011/11/28/can-miley-cyrus-really-help-further-the-occupy-wall-street-cause (accessed January 23, 2012).

44. For videos of some of the religious activities, see Angelo Lopez, "Christians, Jews and Muslims at 'Occupy Wall Street,'" *Everyday Citizen*, October 24, 2011, www.everydaycitizen.com/2011/10/christians_jews_and_muslims_at.html (accessed April 30, 2012).

45. Jane Eisner, "Why 'Occupy Judaism' Is Turning Point," *Forward*, October 13, 2011, http://forward.com/articles/144298/why-occupy-judaism-is-turning-point (accessed April 29, 2012).

46. Catherine Woodiwiss, "Faith Groups Lend Diverse Voices to the Occupy Movement," Center for American Progress, October 25, 2011, www.americanprogress.org/issues/2011/10/occupy_faith_groups.html (accessed April 29, 2012).

47. Rev. Laura Rose, "The Big Interfaith Tent at Occupy Oakland: Faithfully Engaging the 99%," *Huffington Post*, comment posted November 18, 2011, www.huffingtonpost.com/rev-laura-rose/interfaith-occupy-oakland_b_1101997.html (accessed April 29, 2012).

48. John Thavis, "Vatican Calls for Global Authority to Regulate Markets," *National Catholic Reporter*, October 24, 2011, http://ncronline.org/news/global/vatican-calls-global-authority-regulate-markets (accessed April 30, 2012).

49. Cindy Wooden, "Vatican Officials See Agreement in Church Teaching, Occupy Wall Street," *U.S. Catholic*, October 24, 2011, www.uscatholic.org/news/2011/10/vatican-officials-see-agreement-church-teaching-occupy-wall-street (accessed April 30, 2012).

50. Danielle Fleischman and Dan Klein, "'Occupy Wall Street' Movement Brings Jewish Ethos to the Demonstrations," *Jweekly*, October 13, 2011, www.jweekly.com/article/full/63169/occupy-movement-brings-jewish-ethos-to-street (accessed April 29, 2012).

51. Kate Shellnutt, "Occupy Sukkah: Incorporating Jewish Tradition into the Protests," Chron.com, comment posted October 13, 2011, http://blog.chron.com/believeitornot/2011/10/occupy-sukkah-incorporating-jewish-tradition-into-the-protests (accessed January 23, 2012).

52. Jordana Horn, "Occupy Wall Street Jews to 'Occupy Judaism,'" *Jerusalem Post*, October 13, 2011, www.jpost.com/JewishWorld/JewishFeatures/Article.aspx?id=241629 (accessed April 28, 2012).

53. Ibid.

54. Fleischman and Klein, "'Occupy Wall Street' Movement."

55. "Occupy the Occupiers: A Jewish Call for Peace," *Jewish Voice for Peace*, www.youngjewishproud.org/occupy-the-occupiers-a-jewish-call-to-action (accessed April 29, 2012).

56. Peter Fedynsky, "Muslim Groups Back Occupy Wall Street Protesters," *Voice of America*, October 22, 2011, www.voanews.com/english/news/usa/Muslim-Groups-Back-Occupy-Wall-Street-Protesters-132374778.html (accessed April 30, 2012).

57. Lewis Richmond, "Occupy Buddha: Reflections on Occupy Wall Street," *Huffington Post*, comment posted November 28, 2011, www.huffingtonpost.com/lewis-richmond/occupy-buddha_b_1114139.html (accessed April 30, 2012).

58. "UUA President Releases Statement on Occupy Wall Street Protests," in *Voices from the 99 Percent: An Oral History of the Occupy Wall Street Movement*, ed. Lenny Flank (St. Petersburg, FL: Red and Black, 2011), 166.

59. Mardi Tindal, *Occupy Hope*, Wondercafe.ca, comment posted October 22, 2011, www.wondercafe.ca/blogs/moderator-mardi-tindal/occupy-hope (accessed May 4, 2012).

60. "Occupy Faith Statement," *Occupy Faith*, February 28, 2012, www.occupyfaith.com/faith/national-coalition-interfaith-leaders-gather-discuss-role-faith-occupy-wall-st (accessed April 29, 2012).

61. Tom Beaudoin, "Occupy Faith and the Venture of Overlapping Commitments to Practice," *America Magazine*, March 26, 2012, www.americamagazine.org/blog/entry.cfm?entry_id=5017 (accessed April 29, 2012).

62. John Allen, personal interview, New York, April 17, 2012.

63. Stephanie Shockley, personal interview, New York, April 17, 2012.

64. Rita Nakashima Brock, "Why Occupy Oakland Persists in Searching for a Home," *Huffington Post*, comment posted January 30, 2012, www.huffingtonpost.com/rita-nakashima-brock-ph-d/why-occupy-oakland-persists_b_1240784.html (accessed April 29, 2012).

4. THEOLOGY OF THE MULTITUDE

1. Daniel Novick, "Nearly One in Four Residents in Dallas Live in Poverty," CW33.com, February 23, 2012, www.the33tv.com/about/station/newsteam/kdaf-nearly-one-in-four-dallas-residents-live-in-poverty-20120223,0,2234114.story (accessed April 30, 2012).

2. The implications for the middle class are worked out in more detail in Joerg Rieger, *No Rising Tide: Theology, Economics, and the Future* (Minneapolis: Fortress Press, 2009), 34–39 and elsewhere.

3. See, for instance, Stephen G. Hatcher, "The Radicalism of Primitive Methodism," in *Methodist and Radical: Rejuvenating a Tradition*, ed. Joerg Rieger and John Vincent (Nashville, TN: Kingswood Books, 2003).

4. See the instructive book *Evangelicals and Empire: Christian Alternatives to the Political Status Quo*, ed. Bruce Ellis Benson and Peter Goodwin Heltzel (Grand Rapids, MI: Brazos Press, 2008). The various authors point out the different options in the evangelical tradition, which are often overlooked in a context where evangelicalism is seen as identified with the conservative status quo.

5. Néstor Míguez, Joerg Rieger, and Jung Mo Sung, *Beyond the Spirit of Empire: Theology and Politics in a New Key* (London: SCM Press, 2009), 201. It is the voice of the *laos* that "shows the limits of power, returns meaning to the political, puts into play the hope of the excluded, and redeems the human in the creature, and, with it, the whole dimension of creation" (ibid., 202). For more in-depth definitions of *laos* and *demos*, see ibid., 23–24, note 15.

6. *Strong's Concordance*; see http://concordances.org/greek/3793.htm.

7. Ahn Byung Mu, "Jesus and the Minjung in the Gospel of Mark," in *Minjung Theology: People as the Subjects of History*, ed. Kim Yong Bock (Singapore: Commission of Theological Concerns, Christian Conference of Asia, 1981), 140–41.

8. Ibid., 136–40.

9. See Richard A. Horsley, *Jesus and Empire: The Kingdom of God and the New World Disorder* (Minneapolis: Fortress Press, 2003), 51, 129.

10. Michael Hardt and Antonio Negri, *Multitude: War and Democracy in an Age of Empire* (New York: Penguin Press, 2004), 207. In sum, "the multitude is thus composed potentially of all the diverse figures of social production" (ibid., xv). The multitude are "all those who work under the rule of capital and thus potentially as the class of those who refuse the rule of capital" (ibid., 106).

11. Hardt and Negri point out "that the rulers become ever more parasitical and that sovereignty becomes increasingly unnecessary" (ibid., 336).

12. Ibid., 101.

13. Ibid.

14. This phrase was coined by Ernest Hemmingway. For a theological interpretation of grace under pressure, see Joerg Rieger, *Grace under Pressure: Negotiating the Heart of the Methodist Traditions* (Nashville, TN: General Board of Higher Education and Ministry, 2011).

15. For a critique of Adam Smith's notion of the invisible hand of the market and its contemporary uses, see Rieger, *No Rising Tide*, 65–68.

16. Most interpreters are now agreed on the centrality of the covenant and of relationship in the understanding of the biblical notions of justice, both in the Hebrew Bible and in the New Testament. See, for instance, Christopher D. Marshall, *Beyond Retribution: A New Testament Vision for Justice, Crime, and Punishment* (Grand Rapids, MI: Wm. B. Eerdmans, 2001), and Walter Kerber, Claus Westermann, and Bernhard Spörlein, "Gerechtigkeit," in *Christlicher Glaube in moderner Gessellschaft*, Teilband 17 (Freiburg: Herder, 1981).

17. See, for instance, the work of Latin American liberation theologian Leonardo Boff, *Holy Trinity: Perfect Community*, trans. Phillip Berryman (Maryknoll, NY: Orbis Books, 2000); womanist theologian Karen Baker-Fletcher, *Dancing with God: The Trinity from a Womanist Perspective* (St. Louis, MO: Chalice Press, 2006); and Roman Catholic feminist theologian Catherine Mowry LaCugna, *God for Us: The Trinity and Christian Life* (San Francisco: HarperCollins, 1991).

18. Michael Hardt and Antonio Negri, *Commonwealth* (Cambridge, MA: Harvard University Press, 2009), 153. This includes geographical concentration of workers and other resources. In the past, the factory was the site for the working class's production, organization, and rebellion; now the metropolis has taken over these functions (ibid., 250).

19. Ibid., 169.

20. Ibid., 171. Spontaneity and hegemony are not the only alternatives; the multitude can organize "through the conflictual and cooperative interactions of singularities in the common" (ibid., 175).

21. Hardt and Negri, *Multitude*, 212.

22. On this history, see Theodore W. Allen, *The Invention of the White Race*, vol. 2, *The Origin of Racial Oppression in Anglo-America* (London: Verso, 1994).

23. Santiago Slabodsky, "It's *the* History, Stupid! A Dialectical Reading of the Utopian Limitations of the US 'Occupy' Movements," *Peace Studies Journal* 5, no. 1 (January 2012): 48, http://peaceconsortium.org/wp-content/uploads/2010/01/PSJ-Slabodsky-46-561.pdf.

24. Allen, *Invention of the White Race*, 252.

25. Hardt and Negri, *Multitude*, 355.

26. Farid Esack, *Qur'an, Liberation and Pluralism: An Islamic Perspective of Interreligious Solidarity against Oppression* (Oxford: One World, 1997), 99.

27. Ibid., 98. Esack finds this attitude in the Qur'an 7:136–37 and 28:5, both references to the Exodus.

28. Gayatri Chakravorty Spivak, *A Critique of Postcolonial Reason: Toward a History of the Vanishing Present* (Cambridge, MA: Harvard University Press, 1999), 382.

29. Michael Hardt and Antonio Negri, *Empire* (Cambridge, MA: Harvard University Press, 2000), 396.

30. Not only conservative notions of creationism, but also traditional notions of the creator can be troublesome along those lines. James Smith denounces what he considers the multitude's desire for "absolute freedom" over the affirmation of a creator, which rejects simple affirmations of libertarianism and freedom of choice, "insofar as the Creator constitutes the proper Good of the human person" ("The Gospel of Freedom, or Another Gospel?" in *Evangelicals and Empire*, ed. Ellis and Heltzel, 86–89). We do not agree that the multitude's desire for freedom is the same as the libertarian desire for "absolute freedom." And while the divine has a place in defining freedom, this does not have to be envisioned as a top-down deal.

31. Karl Barth's *Church Dogmatics*, vol. 3, part 4, ed. G. W. Bromiley and T. F. Torrance, trans. A. T. Mackay et al. (Edinburgh: T&T Clark, 1961), 544, states that the "command of God" is "a call for the championing of the weak against every kind of encroachment on the part of the strong." Christianity, therefore, needs to keep itself "to the 'left' in opposition to its champions, i.e., to confess that it is fundamentally on the side of the victims."

32. See, for instance, Friedrich-Wilhelm Marquardt's *Theologie und Sozialismus: Das Beispiel Karl Barths* (Munich: Christian Kaiser Verlag, 1972), which argues that this involvement helped shape Barth's theology to a large degree. Part of Marquardt's argument is available in English translation in *Karl Barth and Radical Politics*, ed. and trans. George Hunsinger (Philadelphia: Westminster Press, 1976).

33. Mark Lewis Taylor, "Empire and Transcendence: Hardt and Negri's Challenge to Theology and Ethics," in *Evangelicals and Empire*, ed. Benson and Heltzel, 202. See also his notion of "transimmanence" in Mark Lewis Taylor, *The Theological and the Political: On the Weight of the World* (Minneapolis: Fortress Press, 2011).

34. Barth's notion of transcendence is rooted here as well. Karl Barth, in *Dogmatics in Outline* (New York: Harper & Row, 1959), 40, notes that the highness of God consists in God's descent into the "utter depths of the existence of his creature" in Jesus Christ.

35. John Milbank, "Liberality vs. Liberalism," in *Evangelicals and Empire*, ed. Benson and Heltzel, 102–3.

36. Michael Hardt and Antonio Negri, "Afterword," in *Evangelicals and* Empire, ed. Benson and Heltzel, 311, respond to Milbank by stating that "these capacities of the multitude for self-organization and collective intelligence are what Milbank does not recognize."

37. Hardt and Negri, *Commonwealth*, 15.
38. Hardt and Negri, *Empire*, 157.
39. Ibid.
40. For an argument of how the position of the marginalized can be appreciated in terms of its energy and truth-telling, linked to the divine without having to identify it with the divine, see Joerg Rieger, *Remember the Poor: The Challenge to Theology in the Twenty-First Century* (Harrisburg, PA: Trinity Press International, 1998), chap. 3.
41. The shift from distribution to production is one of the key themes in Rieger, *No Rising Tide*. See also Hardt and Negri, *Commonwealth*, 273. They state, "The question is not, Are people worse off than before? It is rather, Could their abilities and potential be developed more fully?" (ibid., 298).
42. Hardt and Negri, *Multitude*, 100.
43. Ibid., 351.
44. Hardt and Negri comment in *Multitude*, "There is really nothing necessarily metaphysical about the Christian and Judaic love of God: both God's love and humanity's love of God are expressed and incarnated in the common material political project of the multitude" (ibid., 351–52). For theologians, this reminds us of the ongoing task to re-envision the notions of immanence of the transcendence, starting with Jesus' own engagement with the multitude.
45. For the background, see Joerg Rieger, *Christ and Empire: From Paul to Postcolonial Times* (Minneapolis: Fortress Press, 2007), chap. 5. Daniel M. Bell Jr., a theologian of radical orthodoxy, makes a similar distinction between coercion and attraction without being aware that this distinction has long been made in the camp of radical orthodoxy's arch-nemesis, liberal theology. See Daniel M. Bell Jr., "'The Fragile Brilliance of Glass': Empire, Multitude, and the Coming Community," *Political Theology* 11, no. 1 (2012): 69–70.
46. Moltmann says, "The expectation of the great Last Judgment in which the divine justice will triumph was originally a hope cherished by the victims of world history. It was only later that Judgment was understood as punishment imposed on evil-doers" (*The Way of Jesus Christ: Christology in Messianic Dimensions*, trans. Margaret Kohl [Minneapolis: Fortress Press, 1993], 334).
47. Hardt and Negri, *Commonwealth*, 46.

5. REIMAGINING THE GOD OF THE MULTITUDE

1. Frederick Herzog, *God-Walk: Liberation Shaping Dogmatics* (Maryknoll, NY: Orbis Books, 1988), xi.
2. Jennifer Wilder, personal interview, New York, April 17, 2012.
3. Stephanie Shockley, personal interview, New York, April 17, 2012.
4. We thank Seong Joon Park, one of Joerg Rieger's PhD students, for bringing this connection of Jesus and the unemployed to our attention. That this connection was not obvious even to us is further proof of the widespread beholdenness of theology to the status quo.
5. The Confessing Church, of which Bonhoeffer was a part, was not combating secularism, like the so-called Confessing movements in the United States today, but rather a distorted Christianity that had the appearance of being traditional.
6. Frederick Herzog's *God-Walk* uses the terms *Theo-praxis*, *Christo-praxis*, and *Spirit-praxis*.

7. Naomi Wolf, "The Shocking Truth about the Crackdown on Occupy," *Guardian*, November 25, 2011, www.guardian.co.uk/commentisfree/cifamerica/2011/nov/25/shocking-truth-about-crackdown-occupy (accessed May 6, 2012).

8. Anselm of Canterbury, *Proslogion*, trans. M. J. Charlesworth, in *Anselm of Canterbury: The Major Works*, ed. Brian Davies and G. R. Evans (Oxford: Oxford University Press, 1998), 87.

9. On this point there is wide agreement of scholars as different as N. T. Wright, John Dominic Crossan, and Richard A. Horsley.

10. Jürgen Moltmann, *The Way of Jesus Christ: Christology in Messianic Dimensions*, trans. Margaret Kohl (Minneapolis: Fortress Press, 1993), 306.

11. John Wesley, *The Works of the Rev. John Wesley*, ed. Thomas Jackson, 3rd ed. (1872; repr., Peabody, MA: Hendrickson, 1986), 3:178.

12. See John Wesley, "The General Spread of the Gospel," sermon 63, in *The Bicentennial Edition of the Works of John Wesley*, ed. Albert C. Outler (Nashville, TN: Abingdon, 1985), 2:494.

13. For more on Jesus and his heritage of organizing alternatives to empire, see Richard A. Horsley, *Jesus and the Powers: Conflict, Covenant, and the Hope of the Poor* (Minneapolis: Fortress Press, 2010).

14. This is not yet widely recognized. For the historical and exegetical account, see the work of John Dominic Crossan, Richard A. Horsley, Neil Elliott, and Elsa Tamez. For the theological account, see Joerg Rieger, *Christ and Empire: From Paul to Postcolonial Times* (Minneapolis: Fortress Press, 2007), chap. 1.

15. See the numbers presented in chapter 2 of this book.

16. This is one of the key emphases of the work of Friedrich Schleiermacher, father of modern liberal theology.

17. See chapter 4 of this book.

18. Leviticus, however, leaves some loopholes. For instance, slaves from other nations are not subject to liberation (Lev. 25:44–46).

19. Ashgar Ali Engineer, *Islam and Liberation Theology: Essays on Liberative Elements in Islam* (New Delhi: Sterling, 1990), 59. He further states, "And justice is not . . . the rule according to the law laid down by the rich and mighty. Justice, according to the Quran cannot be established as long as the rich and mighty rule."

20. For a more detailed account of the notion of justice along these lines, see Joerg Rieger, *No Rising Tide: Theology, Economics, and the Future* (Minneapolis: Fortress Press, 2009), 134–40.

21. Abuse and violence in families runs frighteningly high. According to statistics presented by the Domestic Violence Resource Center, "Between 600,000 and 6 million women are victims of domestic violence each year, and between 100,000 and 6 million men, depending on the type of survey used to obtain the data." In addition, "studies suggest that between 3.3–10 million children witness some form of domestic violence annually" (www.dvrc-or.org/domestic/violence/resources/C61 [accessed May 7, 2012]).

22. Bartolomé de Las Casas, *The Only Way*, trans. Francis Patrick Sullivan, ed. Helen Rand Parish (New York: Paulist Press, 1992).

23. Marcella Althaus-Reid, *Indecent Theology: Theological Perversions in Sex, Gender, and Politics* (London: Routledge, 2000), 92, 96.

24. Mayra Rivera, *The Touch of Transcendence: A Postcolonial Theology of God* (Louisville, KY: Westminster John Knox Press, 2007), 138. She references Ignacio Ellacuría's statement that "God is transcendent . . . not by being absent, but by being freely present" (ibid., 51).

25. Benjamin Franklin, "Letter to the Abbes Chalut and Arnaud, April 17, 1787," www.revolutionary-war-and-beyond.com/benjamin-franklin-quotations.html (accessed May 7, 2012).

26. Nicholas D. Kristof, "The God Gulf," *New York Times*, January 7, 2004, www.nytimes.com/2004/01/07/opinion/the-god-gulf.html (accessed May 7, 2012).

27. See Leila Ahmed, *A Quiet Revolution: The Veil's Resurgence from the Middle-East to America* (New Haven, CT: Yale University Press, 2011).

28. The initial critique of Latin American liberation theology was addressed not at oppression in general but at such efforts of development.

29. In this regard, Barth's life as a pastor in Safenwil and his support for the blue-collar workers in this town needs to be considered.

30. The Online Quran Project; see www.al-quran.info. Another translation reads, "O you who have believed, be persistently standing firm for Allah, witnesses in justice, and do not let the hatred of a people prevent you from being just. Be just; that is nearer to righteousness. And fear Allah; indeed, Allah is Acquainted with what you do" (www.quran.com).

31. For a fuller account of the Nicene Creed and the resistance against the Roman Empire, see Rieger, *Christ and Empire*, chap. 2.

32. Jürgen Moltmann, *The Crucified God: The Cross of Christ and the Foundation and Criticism of Christian Theology*, trans. R. A. Wilson and John Bowden (New York: Harper & Row, 1974; first published in German in 1972).

33. This is not the ancient modalist heresy of Patripassianism, which held that the Son and the Father suffered in exactly the same fashion, as both were simply modes of the Godhead.

34. Jay Lindsay, "Religion Claims Its Place in Occupy Wall Street," The Associated Press, http://news.yahoo.com/religion-claims-place-occupy-wall-street-171204904.html (accessed May 7, 2012). The quote is attributed to the Rev. Katharine Henderson, president of the Auburn Theological Seminary in New York.

35. See "Presiding Bishop Preaches at Convention Eucharist," Diocese of Missouri, http://news.yahoo.com/religion-claims-place-occupy-wall-street-171204904.html (accessed May 7, 2012).

6. ENVISIONING THE CHURCH OF THE MULTITUDE

1. Leonardo Boff, *Ecclesiogenesis: The Base Communities Reinvent the Church*, trans. Robert R. Barr (Maryknoll, NY: Orbis Books, 1986), 4.

2. Personal interview, Boston, April 3, 2012.

3. Peter C. Hodgson, *Revisioning the Church: Ecclesial Freedom in the New Paradigm* (Philadelphia: Fortress Press, 1988), 24.

4. Ibid., 25.

5. Gerd Theissen, "The Strong and the Weak in Corinth: A Sociological Analysis of a Theological Quarrel," in *The Social Teaching of Pauline Christianity: Essays on Corinth*, ed. and trans. John H. Schütz (Philadelphia: Fortress Press, 1982), 128–29.

6. See, for instance, John Fotopoulos, *Food Offered to Idols in Roman Corinth* (Tübingen: J. C. B. Mohr, 2003), 12–14.

7. Elisabeth Schüssler Fiorenza, *In Memory of Her: A Feminist Theological Reconstruction of Christian Origins* (New York: Crossroad, 1983), 168–78.

8. Elsa Tamez, "The Patriarchal Household and Power Relations between Genders," in *Hope Abundant: Third World and Indigenous Women's Theology*, ed. Kwok Pui-lan (Maryknoll, NY: Orbis Books, 2011), 153.

9. Ibid., 159.

10. Schüssler Fiorenza, *In Memory of Her*, 288.

11. Lewis S. Mudge, *Rethinking the Beloved Community: Ecclesiology, Hermeneutics, Social Theory* (Lanham, MD: University Press of America, 2001), 67–68.

12. Robert B. Ekelund Jr., Robert F. Hébert, and Robert D. Tollison, *The Marketplace of Christianity* (Cambridge, MA: MIT Press, 2006), 94.

13. Ibid., 115.

14. The accepted principle was *cuius regio, eius religio*, meaning that the one who ruled over a certain territory also determined its religion.

15. Max Weber, *The Protestant Ethic and the Spirit of Capitalism*, trans. Talcott Parsons (New York: Scribner, 1958).

16. Ekelund, Hébert, and Tollison, *Marketplace of Christianity*, 190.

17. Ibid., 26.

18. Gustavo Gutiérrez, *A Theology of Liberation: History, Politics, and Salvation*, trans. Caridad Inda and John Eagleson (London: SCM, 1973), chap. 12.

19. Michael Hardt and Antonio Negri, *Empire* (Cambridge, MA: Harvard University Press, 2000), 397.

20. Jessica Firger, "'Occupy' Churches," *Wall Street Journal*, January 12, 2012, http://online.wsj.com/article/SB10001424052970204124204577155090035636750.html (accessed May 12, 2012).

21. BK Hipsher, "Virtual Communion—Real or Not?" unpublished paper, used by permission.

22. See Rachel Wagner, *Godwired: Religion, Ritual and Virtual Reality* (London: Routledge, 2012), 83–86.

23. Ibid., 11.

24. Ibid.

25. Brandon Vogt, *The Church and the New Media: Blogging Converts, Online Activists, and Bishops Who Tweet* (Huntington, IN: Our Sunday Visitor, 2008); Heidi Campbell, *When Religion Meets New Media* (New York: Routledge, 2010).

26. Dietrich Bonhoeffer, *Letters and Papers from Prison*, ed. Eberhard Bethge (New York: Macmillan, 1975), 369–70.

27. Matthew Arlyck, personal interview, New York, April 16, 2012.

28. Paul Tillich, "Kairos und Utopie," in *Gesammelte Werke*, vol. 6, ed. Renate Albrecht (Stuttgart: Evanelgisches Verlagswerk, 1959), 155.

29. Letty M. Russell, *The Church in the Round: Feminist Interpretation of the Church* (Louisville, KY: Westminster John Knox Press, 1993).

30. Ibid., 41.

31. Susan K. Wood, review of *Church in the Round*, by Letty M. Russell, *Modern Theology* 11, no. 3 (1995): 392.

32. Ori Brafman and Rod A. Beckstrom, *The Starfish and the Spider: The Unstoppable Power of Leaderless Organizations* (New York: Portfolio, 2006), 35.

33. Ibid., 46–53.

34. Brian McLaren, *The Church on the Other Side: Doing Ministry in the Postmodern Matrix* (Grand Rapids, MI: Zondervan, 2000); Phyllis Tickle, *The Great Emergence: How Christianity Is Changing and Why* (Grand Rapids, MI: Baker Books, 2008).

35. Fredric Jameson, *Postmodernism, or, the Cultural Logic of Late Capitalism* (Durham, NC: Duke University Press, 1991).

36. Soong-Chan Rah, *The Next Evangelicalism: Freeing the Church from Western Cultural Captivity* (Downers Grove, IL: IVP, 2009), 108–26.

37. Rita Nakashima Brock, phone interview, May 13, 2012.

38. Stuart Murray, *Post-Christendom: Church and Mission in a Strange Land* (Carlisle, Cumbria: Paternoster Press, 2003), 83–88.

39. Ibid., 200–202.

40. L. William Countryman, *Living on the Border of the Holy: Renewing the Priesthood of All* (Harrisburg, PA: Morehouse, 1999), 3.

41. Ibid., 52.

42. Ibid., 66.

43. Brock, phone interview, May 13, 2012.

44. Teresa Berger, "Mapping the Global Struggle for Women's Rites," in *Dissident Daughters: Feminist Liturgies in Global Context* (Louisville, KY: Westminster John Knox Press, 2001), 5.

45. Ibid., 15.

46. Ibid., 22.

47. Grace Yia-Hei Kao, "The Power of Feminist Rituals by Grace Kao," *Feminism and Religion*, March 31, 2012, http://feminismandreligion.com/2012/03/31/the-power-of-feminist-rituals (accessed May 15, 2012).

48. Victor W. Turner, *The Ritual Process: Structure and Anti-Structure* (Chicago: Aldine, 1969).

49. Marcella Althaus-Reid, *The Queer God* (London: Routledge, 2003), 122.

50. Ibid.

51. Bruce Ellis Benson, Malinda Elizabeth Berry, and Peter Goodwin Helzel, "The Just and Peaceful Kingdom," in *Prophetic Evangelicals: Envisioning a Just and Peaceful Kingdom*, ed. Bruce Ellis Benson, Malinda Elizabeth Berry, and Peter Goodwin Helzel (Grand Rapids, MI: Wm. B. Eerdmans, 2012), 9.

52. Catherine Keller and Laurel C. Schneider, eds., *Polydoxy: Theology of Multiplicity and Relation* (London: Routledge, 2011), 153. See the discussion of polydoxy in Kwok Pui-lan, *Globalization, Gender, and Peacebuilding: The Future of Interfaith Dialogue* (Mahwah, NJ: Paulist Press, 2012), 69–77.

53. Jared Cass's presentation at the panel on "Nurturing Cultures of Just-Peace" at the Episcopal Divinity School, Cambridge, Massachusetts, May 2, 2012.

54. Ivone Gebara, *Longing for Running Water: Ecofeminism and Liberation* (Minneapolis: Fortress Press, 1999), 155–62.

55. CB Stewart, personal interview, New York, April 18, 2012.

56. Dr. Martin Luther King Jr., "Beyond Vietnam: A Time to Break Silence," *Information Clearing House*, www.informationclearinghouse.info/article2564.htm (accessed May 16, 2012).

57. Ibid.

58. Christian Smith, "Introduction," in *Disruptive Religion: The Force of Faith in Social-Movement Activism*, ed. Christian Smith (New York: Routledge, 1996), 9–17.

59. Stewart, personal interview, New York, April 18, 2012.

60. Getzel Davis, phone interview, May 14, 2012.

61. David A. M. Wilensky, "Occupy Kol Nidrei NY: 'The Fallacy that Gold Is God,'" *Jewschool*, October 9, 2011, http://jewschool.com/2011/10/09/27069/occupy-kol-nidrei-ny-the-fallacy-that-gold-is-god (accessed May 16, 2012).

Index